NEW IDEAS
FOR
Casseroles

Beatrice Ojakangas

HPBooks®

ANOTHER BEST-SELLING VOLUME FROM HPBooks®

Publisher: Rick Bailey; Editorial Director: Retha M. Davis
Editor: Veronica Durie; Art Director: Don Burton
Typography: Cindy Coatsworth, Michelle Claridge
Book Design: Paul Fitzgerald
Book Manufacture: Anthony B. Narducci
Food Stylist: Carol Flood Peterson; Photography: Cy DeCosse Inc.

Published by HPBooks, Inc.
P.O. Box 5367, Tucson, AZ 85703   602/888-2150
ISBN 0-89586-313-8
Library of Congress Catalog Card Number 84-62581
©1985 HPBooks, Inc. Printed in the U.S.A.
1st Printing

Cover Photo: Chicken Provençal, page 65

Contents

Beatrice Ojakangas

Beatrice Ojakangas, a Finnish American, is the author of nine cookbooks to date, including HP's *Scandinavian Cooking.* Working from her home in Duluth, Minnesota, Beatrice writes on a wide range of cooking subjects for women's magazines and food magazines, appears regularly on local television, teaches cooking and has a weekly food column in a local newspaper.

Beatrice combines her writing and teaching commitments with her responsibilities as the wife of a university professor and mother of three grown children. She finds that when it comes to cooking for the family or a bunch of friends and students, casserole cooking is the way to go! Casseroles have two particular features which make them invaluable to busy people like Beatrice: they can be prepared ahead and they can easily be multiplied to feed large groups. As the oldest of ten children, all living nearby with their families, Beatrice knows about entertaining large numbers! Her recipes include many traditional family dishes and also a number of international casseroles which Beatrice has gathered in her extensive travels.

Casserole Cookery—A Way of Life

Casserole cookery is the way of life for a great number of home cooks. This is true in many parts of the world although we may not always recognize classic foreign dishes as casseroles.

The topic of casseroles breaks down into two essential elements—the dish itself, and the preparation that goes into the dish. There is a variety of casserole dishes available today and more information about them is given on pages 6 and 7.

WHAT IS A CASSEROLE?

A collection of casserole recipes is probably the most valuable part of any good cook's repertoire. Casseroles can be the basis for one-dish menus that range from rustic to fancy fare.

What distinguishes a casserole from any other kind of preparation? One of a casserole's most practical features is that it can usually be prepared, baked, served and stored in the same dish.

Most of the casseroles in this collection can be made ahead. This makes them convenient for people who are short on last-minute preparation time, especially when planning a party. Most casseroles can be covered and refrigerated 24 hours; some can even go to 48 hours. When casseroles are held refrigerated, it is important that they be covered very well. Plastic wrap stretched over the casserole dish and the lid placed on top is double assurance that there will be no drying out or exchange of food flavors. Plastic wrap must be removed before baking. Most casseroles can also be stored in the freezer three to four months if they are well-wrapped.

Refrigerated or thawed frozen casseroles should be baked at the oven temperature indicated in the recipe but usually 15 to 20 minutes longer than stated, or until heated through. To prevent your chilled casserole dish from cracking, place it in a cold oven. This way the dish will heat gradually while the oven heats.

It is important that any food that has been partially cooked be cooled to refrigerator temperature quickly to prevent bacterial growth. Bacteria multiply most quickly at temperatures between 45F and 140F. Casseroles, because of their ingredients, are perfect for bacterial growth, so the sooner you can lower the temperature to below 45F or heat it to above 140F, the safer.

Casseroles have many additional advantages. Many casserole recipes are economical because they stretch expensive ingredients. They are usually easy to serve and lend themselves to casual buffet-style service. Ingredients in a casserole can be flexible as shown in the Basic All-Purpose Casserole Recipe, pages 8 and 9. This flexibility allows you to use leftovers or seasonal extras when you have them.

Menu planning for family or guests is easy when the main dish is a casserole. For most, all that is needed to round out the menu is a fresh salad, good bread, a beverage and a simple dessert.

Not all casseroles in this collection are main dishes. A casserole may make a sole accompaniment to a roast, a barbecued steak, or any other single main course. The casserole can be a vegetable, rice or pasta side dish, appetizer or dessert. Even the bread you serve with the meal can be baked in a casserole.

For everyday and family meals, casseroles solve the problem of the varied-time dinner hour. Casseroles are "forgiving" when they must be made to wait before eating. Sometimes they actually improve on standing. Individual servings of refrigerated casserole leftovers can be put in the microwave for rapid heating.

On days when there has been little time to plan, with a pound of ground meat and a few canned ingredients you can produce a well-balanced, nutritious meal in a short time. Look over the recipes in the Budget Casseroles chapter for those that lend themselves to the emergency shelf.

Many of the casseroles in this collection have an appeal to children and teenagers. Ask them to help you or to cook the whole meal! Try Tamale Pie, page 97, Chili Oven Pancake, page 98, or Baked Tacos, page 101. There are several varieties of lasagna too!

GUIDE TO CASSEROLE DISHES

What do you look for when you buy a casserole dish? Chances are that almost every kitchen has at least one casserole dish. If you were to line up casseroles from every kitchen on one street, the variety would be astonishing.

Casseroles vary in shape and depth, dimension and volume, and the material from which they are made. Each of these variables has an effect on how the casserole will perform.

How do you define a casserole? The renowned encyclopedia of cooking, *Larousse Gastronomique,* describes a casserole as "a cooking utensil made of copper, aluminum, stainless steel, nickel, or other metals, and also of terra cotta, fireproof porcelain, tempered glass and enamelled cast-iron." Larousse goes on to say that deep-sided dishes are the form most common in the United States, and are often used in the oven. The French include in their category of "casseroles" the shallow pans called *sautoirs, sauteuses,* or *plats à sauter,* which are called *skillets* or *frying pans* in most parts of the world.

By using the French definition, almost any utensil in which food is cooked could be called a *casserole.* But, in many parts of the world "casserole" is defined as being a *hot dish* or a *one-dish meal.* We would add that a casserole dish is sturdy enough to be the cooking utensil, yet attractive enough to bring to the table. If it is a deep casserole it often has a lid. Shallow casseroles usually do not.

The recipes in this book indicate the casserole size and specify *deep* or *shallow* when it is important. Volume is indicated in quarts. The composition of the casserole dish is only given in a few cases when a certain material is desirable.

DEPTH OF CASSEROLES

Shallow Casserole—This has a wide surface area in relation to its depth. A greater area of the food surface is exposed to oven heat and there is more moisture evaporation than when a deep casserole is used. Many recipes are especially designed for cooking in a shallow casserole. If the same mixture is cooked in a deep casserole, the resulting food will often be too soupy.

Deep Casserole—This has a specific purpose. Many foods depend on the depth of the casserole

Selection of deep and shallow casserole dishes.

to hold in moisture. Certain foods need moisture to cook properly. These include root vegetables and less-tender cuts of meat. Deep casseroles often have lids which also help to hold in moisture so food will cook properly. The same food cooked in a shallow casserole will be dry and often not cooked through.

WHAT CASSEROLES ARE MADE OF

Glass—Casseroles made of a glass material heat slowly but retain heat longer than other materials. They also cook evenly. Specially treated glass can be used on top of the range and in the oven. Many of these casseroles are inexpensive and easily available. They include clear, colored and white glass. Glass can also be used in the microwave oven.

Enamelled Cast Iron—This is heavy, cooks evenly and can be used both in the oven and on top of the range. Good-quality, enamelled, cast-iron casseroles are expensive. This material cannot be used in the microwave oven.

Steel, Aluminum or Lined Copper—Casseroles made of these materials vary in the evenness of cooking. In general, the heavier the casserole, the more evenly it cooks. It is usually the case that the heavier the casserole, the more expensive it is.

Pottery & Ovenproof Porcelain—These materials have many of the same characteristics as glass but generally cannot be used on top of the range unless specified by the manufacturer. They can mostly be used in the microwave oven. Price varies, depending on the manufacturer. Casseroles made by potters and sold through craft shops may be very expensive, not because of production cost but because of the design. Less-expensive pottery may cook as well but may not be as attractive. Beware of certain inexpensive imported pottery. If you cannot be sure that lead has not been used in the glaze—avoid the product because lead is poisonous.

SIZE OF CASSEROLES

It is important to use the correct size of casserole for the preparation. A casserole dish that is too large will cause the food to dry out. One that is too small risks boiling over and also improper cooking. Most popular sizes range in volume from 1 quart to 3 quart. To measure the volume of a casserole, measure in quarts of water, filling the casserole to the rim.

Casserole dishes of different materials. Top row: Cast Iron; Heavy-Gauge Treated Aluminum; Terra Cotta; Enamelled Cast Iron; center: Lined Copper; Pottery; bottom: Enamelled Steel; Ovenproof Glassware (3 dishes); Ovenproof Porcelain (soufflé dish).

Basic All-Purpose Casserole Recipe

A friend once told me that "a casserole is a blend of inspiration and what's on hand." This basic recipe further illustrates that theory! This is a chart for a "Mix n' Match" casserole. Use this guide to put together inspiration and reality from your pantry.

Protein Ingredient, select 1:
2 cups chopped hard-cooked egg
2 cups diced cooked chicken or turkey
2 cups diced cooked ham
2 cups cooked ground beef
2 cups diced cooked beef or pork
1 lb. fish, cooked, flaked
1 lb. shrimp, cooked
2 (6- to 8-oz.) cans fish or seafood, flaked

Starch Ingredient, select 1:
2 cups uncooked fancy pasta, cooked
1 cup uncooked long-grain white or brown rice, cooked
3 cups uncooked macaroni shells, cooked
4 cups uncooked wide or narrow egg noodles, cooked

Vegetable Ingredient, select 1 or more:
1 (10-oz.) pkg. thawed frozen spinach, broccoli, green beans, Italian beans, green peas, drained
2 cups freshly cooked onion or mushrooms
2 cups diced or sliced fresh zucchini, salted, drained

Sauce Ingredient, select 1:
2 cups Basic White Sauce, opposite
1 (10-1/2-oz.) can cream soup mixed with milk to make 2 cups
1 (16-oz.) can whole or stewed tomatoes with juice

Flavor Ingredients, select 1 or more:
1/4 cup chopped celery
1/4 cup chopped onion
1/4 cup sliced black olives
1 to 2 teaspoons mixed dried leaf herbs, basil, thyme, marjoram, tarragon

Topping/Garnishing Ingredients, select 1 or more:
2 tablespoons grated Parmesan cheese
1/4 cup shredded Swiss, Cheddar or Monterey Jack cheese (1 oz.)
1/4 cup buttered breadcrumbs
1/4 to 1/2 cup canned onion rings
1 to 2 cups frozen, breaded, potato balls

Preheat oven to 350F (175C). Lightly butter a 2- to 2-1/2-quart casserole. Select and prepare a protein ingredient. Select and prepare a starch ingredient. Select and prepare 1 or more vegetable ingredients. Select and prepare a sauce ingredient. Add salt and pepper to taste. Select and prepare 1 or more flavor ingredients. Combine all ingredients in a large bowl or in buttered casserole. Place mixture in casserole. Top with cheese, buttered breadcrumbs, onion rings, potatoes or other crisp ingredient, if desired. Bake, covered, 45 minutes to 1 hour or until heated through. Makes 6 servings.

Basic White Sauce

This is also known as Béchamel Sauce.

1/4 cup butter
1/4 cup all-purpose flour
1/2 teaspoon salt

1/4 teaspoon pepper
1 pint hot milk (2 cups)

In a medium saucepan, melt butter. Stir in flour, salt and pepper. Cook over medium heat, stirring constantly, 3 minutes or until mixture is smooth and bubbly. Whisk in hot milk; bring to a boil, whisking constantly until thickened and smooth. Makes 2 cups.

Chicken Provençal, page 65.

Breakfasts, Brunches & Breads

When does one and one add up to more than two? When you're combining breakfast and lunch! The result is a meal that has such high appeal and versatility that it has become a late-Sunday-morning institution, especially in the United States.

In this chapter there are casseroles that would be marvelous for breakfast, brunch or lunch. Consider them when the house is full of overnight guests. A casserole made ahead and in the refrigerator leaves you free to prepare beverages, set the table, get out the juice or visit with your guests. When you plan the menu around a make-ahead casserole, the greatest part of the work is behind you before the guests arrive.

We often get into a rut. Casseroles for brunch can have a variety of flavors so there is no need to let brunch menus repeat themselves. Choose dishes to echo different international themes such as "Continental," "South-of-the-Border" or "All-American."

Nothing gives more pleasure than the aroma of freshly baked bread, so why not serve your favorite home-baked bread with a leisurely brunch? Almost any yeast bread can be baked in a casserole. The dish itself, especially if made of heavy glass or pottery, gives the exterior of the loaf a crustiness not easily achieved in regular baking pans. Some of the casserole breads are extra appealing because they are quick-to-mix batter breads which require no kneading. The recipe for Casserole Biscuits is especially practical because it requires that you store the yeast dough in the refrigerator in a casserole. You can keep the dough up to 1 week and bake portions of it when needed.

If you convert your favorite recipes to casserole baking, you need to reduce the baking temperature by 25 degrees Fahrenheit. This is the rule when using any glass baking dish. If you do not reduce the temperature, the bread will develop a thick crust before the interior is done.

Casseroles offer a variety of shapes in which to bake breads, from deep rounds to wide flat ovals to shallow square baking dishes. Because of the variation in surface area and thickness of the bread, you will need to check for doneness 10 to 15 minutes earlier when baking in a shallow dish. To check for doneness, insert a wooden skewer into the center of the bread. The skewer should come out clean if the bread is done. You can also check the bread by tapping the bottom with your fingers. A hollow sound means the bread is done. If the exterior of the bread looks dark, lower the oven temperature by another 25 degrees Fahrenheit and/or cover the bread with foil.

Swiss Breakfast or Brunch

Fresh-Fruit Platter
Savory Pots de Crème Suisses, below
Croissants, Butter, Fruit Preserves
Coffee, Tea

◆

Breakfast or Brunch South-of-the-Border

Platter of Assorted Melons with Lime Juice
Tex-Mex Strata, page 17
Hot Corn-Bread Muffins, Butter
Coffee, Tea

◆

All-American Breakfast or Brunch

Baked Apples with Ginger, page 144
Chicken, Artichoke & Mushroom Bake, page 59
Casserole Biscuits, page 19
Butter, Jams, Jellies
Coffee, Tea

Savory Pots de Crème Suisses

Juicy red strawberries and cinnamon muffins are perfect with this!

4 egg yolks
1 pint half and half (2 cups)
1 cup shredded Swiss cheese (4 oz.)

1/4 teaspoon salt
Dash of red (cayenne) pepper

Preheat oven to 300F (150C). In a small bowl, beat egg yolks. In a medium, heavy saucepan, bring half and half just to a simmer. Add cheese, salt and red pepper. Stir until cheese melts. Add a small amount of cheese mixture to egg yolks, then return egg mixture to saucepan. Stir over low heat until blended. Butter 4 individual custard cups. Divide egg mixture between buttered custard cups. Place in a medium baking pan. Add enough hot water to pan to come halfway up sides of custard cups. Bake 15 to 20 minutes or until set in center. Serve warm. Makes 4 servings.

Eggs Baked in Wild-Rice Nests

Flavor of wild rice blends well with lightly baked egg.

2/3 cup uncooked wild rice
2 cups hot water
1 teaspoon salt
1 cup shredded Swiss or
    Jarlsberg cheese (4 oz.)
8 eggs

2 tablespoons butter
8 smoky, fully cooked, link sausages,
    sliced
1/2 cup whipping cream
1/2 cup fresh breadcrumbs
1 tablespoon butter, melted

Rinse wild rice in 3 changes of hot tap water or until water is no longer cloudy. In a medium saucepan, bring 2 cups water and salt to a boil; stir in rice. Bring back to a boil. Cover and reduce heat to low. Cook 35 minutes or until rice is tender and has absorbed all the liquid. Preheat oven to 350F (175C). Butter a shallow 1-1/2-quart casserole, or 11" x 7" or 8-inch-square baking dish. Spread rice over bottom of buttered casserole. Sprinkle with 1/2 of cheese. Make 8 evenly spaced indentations in rice and cheese. Carefully crack 1 egg into each indentation. Pierce egg yolks but do not stir; dot with 2 tablespoons butter. Arrange sausage slices around eggs. Pour cream over all. Sprinkle with remaining cheese. In a small bowl, combine breadcrumbs and 1 tablespoon melted butter; sprinkle over cheese in casserole. Bake, uncovered, 15 to 25 minutes or until cheese is melted and eggs are set to your liking. Makes 4 servings.

Mushroom Brunch Casserole

Great for a Sunday brunch with sliced melon and fresh muffins.

2 tablespoons butter
8 oz. fresh mushrooms, sliced
1 bunch green onions, chopped
1 medium, green bell pepper,
    chopped, if desired
12 slices 7-grain or whole-wheat bread,
    crusts removed
2 cups shredded Cheddar cheese (8 oz.)

8 eggs, beaten
3 cups milk
1 tablespoon chopped fresh parsley
1 teaspoon Dijon-style mustard
1 teaspoon salt
1/4 teaspoon black pepper
10 bacon slices, crisp-cooked, crumbled
1 tomato, peeled, seeded, diced

Generously butter a shallow 3-quart casserole or 13" x 9" baking dish. In a large skillet, melt butter. Add mushrooms, green onions and green pepper, if desired; sauté about 10 minutes or until liquid has evaporated. Remove from heat. Arrange 6 bread slices in bottom of buttered casserole. Top with 1/2 of cheese, all mushroom mixture, then with remaining bread slices. Top bread with remaining cheese. In a large bowl, beat eggs, milk, parsley, mustard, salt and black pepper. Pour over bread mixture in casserole. Sprinkle bacon and tomato evenly over top. Cover and refrigerate several hours or overnight. Preheat oven to 325F (165C). Bake, uncovered, 50 minutes to 1 hour or until a knife inserted in center comes out clean. Let stand 5 minutes before serving. Makes 12 servings.

How to Make Eggs Baked in Wild-Rice Nests

1/Make 8 evenly spaced indentations in rice and cheese. Carefully crack 1 egg into each indentation. Pierce egg yolks but do not stir; dot with butter.

2/Arrange sausage slices around eggs. Pour cream over all. Sprinkle with cheese and buttered breadcrumbs. Bake until cheese is melted and eggs are set.

Egg Scramble with Turkey Ham

Turkey ham has fewer calories than ham made from pork.

6 thick bread slices, crusts removed, cubed
1 lb. turkey ham, cut in 1/2-inch cubes
8 oz. Cheddar cheese, cubed
8 eggs, beaten

1 pint milk (2 cups)
1/2 teaspoon dried leaf thyme
1/2 teaspoon dry mustard

The day before you plan to serve this casserole, butter a shallow 3-quart casserole or 13'' x 9'' baking dish. Sprinkle bread cubes, turkey ham and cheese evenly over bottom of buttered casserole. In a large bowl, beat eggs, milk, thyme and mustard. Pour egg mixture over ham mixture in casserole. Cover and refrigerate overnight. Preheat oven to 325F (165C). Bake casserole, uncovered, 1 hour or until edges are lightly browned and a knife inserted in center comes out clean. Makes 8 servings.

Baked Artichoke & Shrimp Omelet

Artichokes and shrimp add elegance as well as flavor!

1 (9-oz.) pkg. frozen artichoke hearts or
   1 (8-1/2-oz. net dr. wt.) can artichoke
   hearts
6 eggs
1/2 teaspoon salt
1/8 teaspoon red (cayenne) peper
2 tablespoons olive oil

3/4 cup chopped green onion
1 cup cooked peeled shrimp
1/2 cup whipping cream
3/4 cup shredded Swiss or
   Jarlsberg cheese (3 oz.)
1/4 cup grated Parmesan cheese (3/4 oz.)

Preheat oven to 400F (205C). Butter a 1-1/2-quart casserole or quiche dish. Cook frozen artichoke hearts according to package directions; drain. Rinse, drain and quarter canned artichoke hearts. In a medium bowl, beat eggs, salt and red pepper. In a medium skillet, heat oil. Add green onion; sauté 5 minutes or until wilted. Add artichokes; sauté 2 to 3 minutes longer. Remove from heat; add shrimp and cream. Pour into egg mixture; mix well. Pour into buttered casserole. Sprinkle with cheeses. Bake, uncovered, 15 to 20 minutes or until a knife inserted in center comes out clean. Makes 4 servings.

Swiss Egg & Cheese Bake

You'll find this a delicious and practical dish when you have Sunday-morning guests!

6 eggs
1/3 cup milk
1/2 teaspoon salt
1/4 teaspoon white pepper
1 teaspoon dried leaf tarragon

2 tablespoons butter
1 cup diced cooked ham (4 oz.)
1 cup shredded Swiss or
   Gruyère cheese (4 oz.)
1/4 cup fine fresh breadcrumbs

Preheat oven to 400F (205C). Butter a shallow 1- to 1-1/2-quart casserole or 8-inch-square baking dish. In a medium bowl, beat eggs, milk, salt, white pepper and tarragon. In a large skillet, melt butter. Add egg mixture. Cook and stir over medium heat until just starting to set. Spoon mixture into buttered casserole. Sprinkle with ham, cheese and breadcrumbs. Bake, uncovered, 10 minutes or until top is golden. Makes 6 servings.

Baked Artichoke & Shrimp Omelet, above, and Three-Grain Bread, page 21.

Chicken Casserole with Water Chestnuts

Substitute cooked turkey for the chicken if you wish.

1 (3-1/2-lb.) chicken, whole or cut up
Water
1 teaspoon salt
9 thick bread slices
1/4 cup butter
8 oz. fresh mushrooms, sliced
1 (8-oz.) can sliced water chestnuts, drained
1 (2-oz.) jar sliced pimentos, drained

1/2 cup mayonnaise
9 slices Cheddar cheese
1/4 cup all-purpose flour
4 eggs, well beaten
1 pint milk (2 cups)
1-1/2 teaspoons salt
Buttered Breadcrumbs, see below

Buttered Breadcrumbs:
Crusts from bread slices, above

1/4 cup butter, melted

Place chicken in a large saucepan. Add water just to cover and salt. Simmer 30 to 45 minutes or until chicken is tender. Cool in broth. Drain chicken, reserving broth. Measure 2 cups broth; set aside. Remove and discard skin and bones from chicken. Cut meat into 1-inch pieces to give about 4 cups. Trim crusts from bread slices and reserve to prepare Buttered Breadcrumbs. Lightly butter a shallow 3-quart casserole or 13" x 9" baking dish. Line bottom of buttered casserole with crustless bread slices making a single layer. Top bread with cooked chicken pieces. In a large skillet, melt 2 tablespoons butter. Add mushrooms; sauté 5 minutes or until lightly browned. Sprinkle mushrooms over chicken in casserole. Sprinkle water chestnuts and pimentos over mushroom layer. Dot with mayonnaise and top with cheese. Melt remaining 2 tablespoons butter in skillet. Stir in flour until smooth. Whisk in reserved 2 cups chicken broth. Bring to a boil, whisking constantly until thickened and smooth; set aside. In a medium bowl, beat eggs, milk and salt. Pour over cheese layer in casserole. Spoon chicken-broth sauce over all. Cover and re-frigerate overnight. Prepare Buttered Breadcrumbs. Preheat oven to 350F (175C). Just before baking, sprinkle casserole with Buttered Breadcrumbs. Bake, uncovered, 1 to 1-1/2 hours or until a knife inserted in center comes out clean. Makes 12 servings.

Buttered Breadcrumbs:
Using a food processor fitted with a steel blade or a blender, make crumbs from bread crusts. Measure 2 cups. In a large skillet, melt butter; add breadcrumbs. Toast over low heat 10 to 15 minutes or until dry, stirring occasionally. Makes 2 cups.

Do not store cooked chicken or turkey without freezing for more than three days. Freeze in convenient quantities, such as 2-cup amounts, to allow faster thawing.

Tex-Mex Strata

Corn tortillas take the place of bread in this strata.

8 oz. fresh bulk pork sausage, mild,
   regular or hot
2/3 cup chopped green onion
1/3 cup chopped green bell pepper
12 (6-inch) corn tortillas
1-1/2 cups shredded Cheddar cheese (6 oz.)

1 cup shredded Monterey Jack cheese (4 oz.)
1 pint milk (2 cups)
4 eggs, beaten
1/2 teaspoon salt
1/2 cup tomato sauce
1 (4-oz.) can diced green chilies

Butter an 8-inch-square baking dish. In a large skillet, cook sausage, green onion and green pepper until sausage is crumbly and no longer pink. Drain off fat; set sausage mixture aside. Arrange 4 tortillas in bottom of buttered baking dish. Sprinkle with 1/2 of sausage mixture and 1/2 of Cheddar cheese. Top with 4 more tortillas, remaining sausage mixture and remaining Cheddar cheese. Top with remaining tortillas. Press tortillas down firmly over layers to remove air spaces and even out mixture in dish. Top with Monterey Jack cheese. In a medium bowl, beat milk, eggs, salt, tomato sauce and green chilies. Pour over layers in baking dish. Cover and refrigerate several hours or overnight. Remove from refrigerator 1 hour before baking. Preheat oven to 325F (165C). Bake, uncovered, 40 to 45 minutes or until a knife inserted near center comes out clean. Let stand 10 minutes before serving. Makes 6 servings.

Early American Spoon Bread

Spoonbread is so named because you spoon it to serve.

1 pint milk (2 cups)
2 tablespoons butter
1 teaspoon sugar
1/2 teaspoon salt

2/3 cup yellow cornmeal
4 eggs, separated
Melted butter

Preheat oven to 350F (175C). Butter a deep 1-1/2-quart casserole or soufflé dish. In a medium saucepan, combine milk, 2 tablespoons butter, sugar, salt and cornmeal. Bring to a boil, stirring constantly. Cook and stir until thick and smooth. Quickly stir in egg yolks until blended; set aside. In a medium bowl, beat egg whites until soft peaks form. Fold egg whites into cornmeal mixture. Turn into buttered casserole. Bake 30 to 35 minutes or until puffy and set. Serve immediately with melted butter to pour over individual servings. Makes 6 servings.

Wheat Monkey Bread

This pull-apart loaf is easy to serve.

1 cup milk
1/4 cup warm water (110F, 45C)
1 (1/4-oz.) pkg. active dry yeast
    (1 tablespoon)
2 tablespoons sugar
1-1/2 teaspoons salt
2 tablespoons butter, room temperature

2 eggs
1-1/2 cups whole-wheat flour
2 to 2-1/2 cups unbleached
    all-purpose flour
1/2 cup butter, melted
1 cup wheat germ

Generously butter a 2-quart casserole. In a small saucepan, heat milk until bubbles form around edge of pan. Remove from heat; cool to 110F (45C) or until a few drops on your wrist feel warm. Pour warm water into a large bowl; stir in yeast and sugar until dissolved. Let stand until foamy, about 5 minutes. Stir in salt, cooled milk, 2 tablespoons room-temperature butter, eggs and whole-wheat flour; beat well. Gradually add all-purpose flour, beating to keep mixture smooth. Add enough all-purpose flour to give a stiff dough. Let dough rest 15 minutes. Turn out dough onto a lightly floured surface. Clean and butter bowl. Knead dough 10 minutes or until smooth and satiny, adding all-purpose flour as necessary to keep dough from sticking. Place dough in buttered bowl, turning to coat all sides. Cover and let rise in a warm place until doubled in size, about 1 hour. Turn out dough onto a lightly oiled surface. Divide dough into quarters. Divide each quarter into quarters to make 16 pieces. Divide each piece into 2 parts, making a total of 32 pieces. Place melted butter and wheat germ in 2 separate small dishes. Roll each piece of dough in melted butter, then roll in wheat germ. Place dough pieces in even layers in buttered casserole. Cover and let rise in a warm place until doubled in size, 45 minutes to 1 hour. Preheat oven to 375F (190C). Bake 35 to 45 minutes or until a skewer inserted in center comes out clean. Cool in casserole 5 minutes. Invert onto a serving dish. Pull apart pieces to serve. Makes 32 pull-apart rolls.

Custard Corn Bake

Try this with maple syrup poured over each serving.

3 eggs
1 qt. milk (4 cups)
1 teaspoon salt
1 cup yellow cornmeal

2 teaspoons baking powder
1 tablespoon sugar
2 tablespoons vegetable oil

Preheat oven to 375F (190C). Butter a deep 2-quart casserole. In a large bowl, beat eggs, milk and salt. In another large bowl, mix cornmeal, baking powder and sugar. Stir oil and 1/2 of egg mixture into cornmeal mixture until blended. Turn into buttered casserole. Pour remaining egg mixture over mixture in casserole. Bake, uncovered, stirring 3 times during first 15 minutes. Bake 45 minutes longer or until top is golden and crust has formed. Makes 6 servings.

How to Make Wheat Monkey Bread

1/Divide dough into quarters. Divide each quarter into quarters to make 16 pieces. Divide each piece into 2 parts, making a total of 32 pieces. Roll each piece of dough in melted butter, then in wheat germ.

2/Place dough pieces in even layers in casserole. Cover and let rise until doubled in size. Bake 35 to 45 minutes.

Casserole Biscuits

You can keep this biscuit dough refrigerated in a casserole for one week.

1/4 cup warm water (110F, 45C)
2 (1/4-oz.) pkgs. active dry yeast
   (2 tablespoons)
5 cups self-rising flour

1/3 cup sugar
1 teaspoon baking soda
1 cup shortening
1 pint buttermilk (2 cups)

Pour warm water into a small bowl; stir in yeast until dissolved. Let stand until foamy, about 5 minutes. In a large bowl, mix flour, sugar and baking soda. Using a pastry cutter or 2 knives, cut in shortening until mixture resembles coarse crumbs. Stir in yeast mixture and buttermilk; mix well. Turn into a medium casserole. Cover and refrigerate at least 2 hours before using. Remove desired amount of dough from casserole. On a lightly floured surface, roll out dough 1/2 inch thick; cut into 2-inch rounds, squares, crescents or triangles. Place biscuits on an unbuttered or parchment-lined baking sheet. Let rise in a warm place until doubled in size, about 2 hours. Preheat oven to 450F (230C). Bake 10 minutes or until golden. Makes about 48 (2-inch) biscuits.

Cinnamon Bubble Bread

As delicious as cinnamon rolls, but quicker to prepare.

1 cup milk
1 cup warm water (110F, 45C)
2 (1/4-oz.) pkgs. active dry yeast
  (2 tablespoons)
2 tablespoons sugar
2 teaspoons salt

2 tablespoons butter, melted
4-1/2 cups all-purpose flour
1/2 cup butter, melted
1/2 cup sugar
1 tablespoon ground cinnamon

Generously butter a deep 2-quart casserole. In a small saucepan, heat milk until bubbles form around edge of pan. Remove from heat; cool to 110F (45C) or until a few drops on your wrist feel warm. Pour warm water into a large bowl; stir in yeast and 2 tablespoons sugar until dissolved. Let stand until foamy, about 5 minutes. Add salt, cooled milk, 2 tablespoons butter and 1 cup flour; beat until smooth. Gradually beat in remaining flour to make a stiff, satiny, smooth dough. Cover and let rise in a warm place until doubled in size, about 45 minutes. Turn out dough onto a lightly oiled surface. Divide dough into quarters. Divide each quarter into quarters to make 16 pieces. Divide each piece into 2 parts, making a total of 32 pieces. Place 1/2 cup melted butter in a small dish. In another small dish, mix 1/2 cup sugar and cinnamon. Roll each piece of dough in melted butter, then in cinnamon sugar. Place dough pieces in even layers in buttered casserole. Cover and let rise in a warm place until doubled in size, about 45 minutes. Preheat oven to 375F (190C). Bake 35 to 45 minutes or until browned and a skewer inserted in center comes out clean. Cool in casserole 5 minutes. Invert onto a serving dish. Pull apart pieces to serve. Makes 32 pull-apart rolls.

Cinnamon Sally Lunn

A cake-like bread, created by Sally Lunn in 18th-century Bath, England.

2 (1/4-oz.) pkgs. active dry yeast
  (2 tablespoons)
1/4 cup sugar
5 cups unbleached all-purpose flour
1-1/2 teaspoons salt

1 pint hot milk (125F, 50C, 2 cups)
2 eggs, slightly beaten
1/3 cup butter, melted
Ground cinnamon

In the large bowl of an electric mixer, combine yeast, sugar, 2 cups flour and salt. Add hot milk; beat at high speed with electric mixer until mixture is smooth and satiny. Add eggs, butter and remaining flour; beat with mixer until smooth. If batter is too stiff for mixer, beat 100 strokes by hand using a wooden spoon. Cover and let rise in a warm place until doubled in size, about 1 hour. Generously butter a deep 2-1/2-quart casserole or 10-inch tube pan. Generously sprinkle inside with cinnamon so entire surface is dusted. Stir down batter. Turn into prepared casserole. Let rise in a warm place until batter is within 1 inch of top of pan, about 45 minutes. Preheat oven to 350F (175C). Bake 45 minutes or until bread sounds hollow when tapped with your fingers. Turn bread out of casserole and serve hot. Makes 1 large loaf.

Three-Grain Bread   Photo on page 15.

This nutritious bread makes a large crusty loaf.

2 cups warm water (110F, 45C)
1 (1/4-oz.) pkg. active dry yeast
  (1 tablespoon)
3 tablespoons dark molasses
1 cup nonfat-milk powder
2 tablespoons butter, room temperature
2 teaspoons salt

1/2 cup quick-cooking or
  regular rolled oats
1/2 cup dark rye flour
1-1/4 cups whole-wheat flour
2-1/2 cups unbleached all-purpose flour
Additional rolled oats

Pour warm water into a large bowl; stir in yeast and molasses until dissolved. Let stand until foamy, about 3 minutes. Stir in milk powder, butter, salt, 1/2 cup oats, rye flour and whole-wheat flour; beat until smooth. Beat in all-purpose flour until batter is stiff and smooth. Cover and let rise in a warm place until doubled in size, about 1 hour. Generously butter a deep 2-1/2-quart casserole. Sprinkle with additional oats. Turn batter into prepared casserole. Sprinkle more oats over batter. Let rise in a warm place until doubled in size, about 1 hour. Preheat oven to 350F (175C). Bake 45 minutes or until bread sounds hollow when tapped with your fingers. Cool in casserole on a rack 10 minutes. Turn out bread and cool on rack. Makes 1 large loaf.

Caraway-Onion-Oat Bread

To make a rye bread, substitute rye flour for the rolled oats.

1 cup milk
1/2 cup dairy sour cream
2 teaspoons salt
3 tablespoons dark-brown sugar
3 tablespoons butter, melted
1/2 cup warm water (110F, 45C)
2 (1/4-oz.) pkgs. active dry yeast
  (2 tablespoons)

2 eggs
1 tablespoon caraway seeds
1 cup chopped green onion
1/2 cup chopped fresh parsley
1-1/2 cups regular or
  quick-cooking rolled oats
4 to 5 cups unbleached all-purpose flour
Additional rolled oats

In a medium saucepan, heat milk and sour cream to 150F (65C). Stir in salt, sugar and butter. Cool to room temperature, about 30 minutes. Pour warm water into a small bowl; stir in yeast until dissolved. Let stand until foamy, about 5 minutes. In a large bowl, beat eggs. Stir in milk mixture, yeast mixture, caraway seeds, green onion and parsley. Stir in 1-1/2 cups oats and 1 cup flour; beat with a wooden spoon until mixture is glossy. Stir in remaining flour until mixture is stiff. Cover and let rest 15 minutes. Turn out dough onto a lightly floured surface. Clean and butter bowl; set aside. Knead dough 10 minutes or until smooth and elastic. Place dough in buttered bowl, turning to coat all sides. Cover and let rise in a warm place until doubled in size, about 1-1/2 hours. Generously butter 2 deep 1-1/2-quart casseroles. Sprinkle with additional oats. Punch down dough; cut into 2 parts. Shape each part into a smooth round loaf. Place 1 loaf in each buttered casserole. Cover and let rise in a warm place until dough fills casseroles, about 45 minutes. Preheat oven to 350F (175C). Bake 35 to 40 minutes or until bread sounds hollow when tapped with your fingers. Turn bread out of casseroles. Cool on racks. Makes 2 loaves.

Appetizers

By definition, appetizers are any food that stimulates the appetite. A thoughtful host or hostess will serve just enough to whet guests' tastes for the meal to come. Preparing appetizers in a casserole helps you to organize and save time. All of them can be assembled ahead and refrigerated before heating to serve. Serving is easy. Many appetizers have dramatic, spicy flavors but can provide good nutrition as well.

For a minimum of last-minute fuss, an all-appetizer buffet party can serve as a meal, and is a pleasant way to serve guests over a span of hours. Try an appetizer buffet for the neighborhood. All of these appetizers can be assembled ahead. It is helpful to have a warming tray to keep them warm if you plan to serve throughout an evening. If your party will span more than 2 hours, plan to have an extra "refresher" or alternate casserole ready to heat and serve. This will prevent holding food too long at room temperature or at temperatures that might encourage bacterial growth, between 45F and 140F.

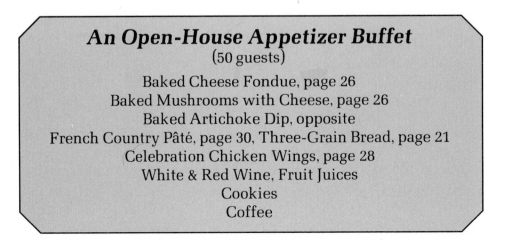

An Open-House Appetizer Buffet
(50 guests)

Baked Cheese Fondue, page 26
Baked Mushrooms with Cheese, page 26
Baked Artichoke Dip, opposite
French Country Pâté, page 30, Three-Grain Bread, page 21
Celebration Chicken Wings, page 28
White & Red Wine, Fruit Juices
Cookies
Coffee

Baked Artichoke Dip

Bake this zesty dip in a pretty oven-to-table casserole.

1 (8-1/2-oz. net dr. wt.) can artichoke
   hearts, drained, rinsed
1 cup grated Parmesan cheese (3 oz.)
1 cup mayonnaise
1 garlic clove, minced

1 tablespoon lemon juice
1 teaspoon Dijon-style mustard
1/2 teaspoon salt
Dash of hot-pepper sauce
Assorted raw vegetables or crackers

Preheat oven to 400F (205C). Butter a 3- to 4-cup casserole. Drain artichokes well, squeezing out all liquid; cut into quarters. Place quartered artichokes, Parmesan cheese, mayonnaise, garlic, lemon juice, mustard, salt and pepper sauce in a food processor fitted with a steel blade. Process until artichokes are finely chopped but not pureed. If desired, chop artichokes by hand, then combine with remaining ingredients except raw vegetables or crackers. Spoon mixture into buttered casserole. Bake, uncovered, 15 minutes or until lightly browned. Serve hot with assorted raw vegetables or crackers for dipping. Makes 2 cups.

Chile con Queso

This translates to chilies with cheese.

2 tablespoons butter
1 small onion, minced
1 (14- to 15-oz.) can whole tomatoes, cut up
1 (4-oz.) can diced green chilies
1 (8-oz.) pkg. cream cheese, cubed

1/2 pint whipping cream (1 cup)
1 cup shredded Monterey Jack cheese (4 oz.)
Assorted raw vegetables
Tortilla chips

Preheat oven to 350F (175C). In a small skillet, melt butter. Add onion; sauté 5 minutes or until tender. Turn into a 1-1/2-quart casserole. Add tomatoes with juice, green chilies, cream cheese and cream. Bake, uncovered, 30 minutes or until bubbly. Sprinkle with Monterey Jack cheese. Serve immediately with assorted raw vegetables and tortilla chips for dipping. Makes 10 servings.

Add a little variety to the selection of dipping vegetables by using some of the following cut into sticks or slices where appropriate: green bell peppers; turnips; zucchini; cucumber; jícama; fresh mushrooms; edible pea pods; cauliflowerets; broccoli flowerets; rutabaga; Belgian endive; hearts of romaine.

Curried Mushrooms

This appetizer can also be a first course served with rice.

1/4 cup butter
2 cups chopped onion (about 2 large)
2 garlic cloves, minced
1 cup chopped celery
1-1/2 lbs. fresh mushrooms
1-1/2 teaspoons salt
1 teaspoon each ground cumin,
    ground cinnamon, ground turmeric and
    ground ginger
1/2 teaspoon dry mustard

1/2 teaspoon ground cloves
2 large cooking apples, peeled, chopped
3 large tomatoes, peeled, seeded, chopped
3 tablespoons shredded coconut
1 tablespoon honey
2 tablespoons lemon juice
Crisp toast rounds or cooked plain or
    wild rice
Toasted sliced almonds

Preheat oven to 350F (175C). In a large skillet, melt butter. Add onion and garlic; sauté 5 minutes or until tender. Turn into a 2-quart casserole. Add celery. Remove caps from mushrooms. Chop mushroom stems. Stir chopped stems, mushroom caps and salt into casserole. Bake, covered, 30 minutes or until mushrooms have released juices. While mushroom mixture cooks, in a small bowl, mix cumin, cinnamon, turmeric, ginger, mustard and cloves. Stir into mushroom mixture with apples, tomatoes, coconut, honey and lemon juice. Bake, uncovered, 25 minutes or until all ingredients are just tender; do not overcook. Cover and let stand 10 minutes before serving. Serve on crisp toast rounds or over cooked plain or wild rice. Garnish with almonds. Makes 12 servings.

Baked Broccoli & Parmesan Dip

Try this also as a broiled topping for lean hamburgers!

1 (10-oz.) pkg. frozen chopped broccoli or
    1 lb. fresh broccoli
1 cup mayonnaise
1 tablespoon lemon juice
1 tablespoon dried leaf basil
1 teaspoon chili powder

1/2 cup chopped chives
1/2 cup chopped fresh parsley
1 cup grated Parmesan cheese (3 oz.)
Melba toast, crackers or
    assorted raw vegetables

Preheat oven to 350F (175C). Cook frozen broccoli according to package directions; drain. If using fresh broccoli, cut off and discard tough ends from stalks. Peel remaining stalks if skin is tough. Cook in boiling water 20 minutes or until tender; drain. Finely chop broccoli. In a medium bowl, combine broccoli, mayonnaise, lemon juice, basil, chili powder, chives, parsley and Parmesan cheese. Turn into a shallow 1-quart casserole. Bake, uncovered, 20 minutes or until heated through and browned on top. Serve with Melba toast, crackers or assorted raw vegetables for dipping. Makes 12 to 15 servings.

Curried Mushrooms, above; Celebration Chicken Wings, page 28; and Baked Broccoli & Parmesan Dip, above.

Baked Mushrooms with Cheese

Use wild morels in place of white mushrooms if you have them!

7 tablespoons butter
1 lb. fresh mushrooms, sliced
1/4 teaspoon ground nutmeg
Salt and pepper to taste
1/4 cup whipping cream

6 to 8 slices French bread,
  cut 1 inch thick
1/2 cup shredded Gruyère or
  other Swiss cheese (2 oz.)
Chopped fresh parsley

Preheat oven to 400F (205C). In a large skillet, melt butter. Add mushrooms; sauté 10 minutes or until liquid has evaporated. Reduce heat to medium low; stir in nutmeg, salt, pepper and cream. Cook until thickened. Arrange bread slices in a shallow 1-1/2-quart casserole or 8-inch-square baking dish. Make a slight indentation in the middle of each slice. Spoon mushroom mixture over slices; sprinkle with cheese. Bake, uncovered, 10 minutes or until cheese is melted. Garnish with parsley. Makes 6 to 8 servings.

Baked Cheese Fondue

When you bake a cheese fondue there is little last-minute fuss!

1 garlic clove, cut in half
1 cup dry white wine
1 tablespoon lemon juice
4 cups shredded Swiss, Jarlsberg,
  or Gruyère cheese (1 lb.)

3 tablespoons all-purpose flour
3 tablespoons kirsch
Ground nutmeg to taste
2 loaves crusty French bread, cut in cubes

Preheat oven to 425F (220C). In a deep 2-quart crockery casserole, combine garlic, wine and lemon juice. In a medium bowl, toss cheese with flour; stir into wine mixture. Bake 30 to 40 minutes or until cheese is melted, stirring once or twice during baking. Stir in kirsch and nutmeg until smooth. Place over a fondue burner to keep hot. Give guests fondue forks. Serve with French-bread cubes for dipping. Makes 8 to 12 servings.

Kirsch is a colorless brandy distilled from the fermented juice of black cherries.

How to Make Baked Mushrooms with Cheese

1/Arrange bread slices in a shallow 1-1/2-quart casserole. Make a slight indentation in the middle of each slice.

2/Spoon mushroom mixture over bread slices; sprinkle with cheese. Bake until cheese is melted.

Creamy Baked Raclette

Raclette cheese is usually broiled but it's great baked with cream!

**8 oz. aged Raclette, Swiss or
   Jarlsberg cheese**

**3 tablespoons whipping cream
Crusty French bread or hot boiled potatoes**

Preheat oven to 400F (205C). Cut cheese into slices about 1/3 inch thick. Place in a small shallow casserole, gratin dish or 8-inch pie pan in a single layer or slightly overlapping. Drizzle with cream. Bake, uncovered, 10 to 15 minutes or until cheese is bubbly and begins to brown around edges. Serve immediately with crusty French bread for dipping or over hot boiled potatoes. Makes about 6 servings.

Celebration Chicken Wings   *Photo on page 25.*

Save and freeze chicken wings to use in this recipe.

10 lbs. chicken wings, disjointed
1-1/2 cups Japanese-style soy sauce
1-1/2 cups sweet sherry
2/3 cup sugar
10 garlic cloves, minced
1 whole piece gingerroot,
   shredded (about 4 oz.)
20 red hot Szechwan peppers,
   include seeds and pods

2/3 cup red-wine vinegar
2/3 cup ketchup
2-1/2 cups chicken broth
1/4 cup cornstarch
Chopped fresh cilantro (coriander),
   if desired

Wash chicken wings; pat dry with paper towels. Remove and discard wing-tips or save for broth. Place remaining wing pieces in a large bowl. In a medium bowl, combine soy sauce, sherry, sugar, garlic, gingerroot, peppers, vinegar, ketchup and chicken broth. Pour over chicken wings. Cover and refrigerate at least 4 hours or overnight to marinate. Remove wings from marinade, reserving marinade. Arrange wings close together in a single layer in a large shallow casserole. Use several casseroles if necessary. Drizzle with enough marinade to moisten. Preheat oven to 400F (205C). Bake, uncovered, 30 to 40 minutes or until wings are tender. Remove to another large casserole or pile on a large platter. In a small saucepan, blend chicken cooking juices, reserved marinade and cornstarch. Bring to a boil. Cook, stirring constantly, until thickened. Pour over wings. Sprinkle with cilantro, if desired. Serve hot or at room temperature. Makes about 150 wing pieces.

Deviled Chicken Wings

Chilled, this is perfect finger food for a picnic.

2 lbs. chicken wings, disjointed
1 to 2 dried, small, red chilies
1/4 cup dark soy sauce
1/3 cup sweet sherry
1 teaspoon sugar
1 garlic clove, bruised, peeled
1 slice fresh gingerroot,
   about 1/8 inch thick

1/4 cup water
2 teaspoons cornstarch
2 teaspoons water
1/2 teaspoon sesame oil
1 tablespoon Dijon-style mustard

Preheat oven to 300F (150C). Wash chicken wings; pat dry with paper towels. Remove and discard wing-tips or save for broth. Place remaining wing pieces in a shallow 3-quart casserole or 13'' x 9'' baking dish. Crumble chilies, using seeds and pod. In a small saucepan, combine soy sauce, sherry, sugar, garlic, gingerroot, chilies and 1/4 cup water; bring just to a boil. Pour over chicken wings. Bake, uncovered, 45 minutes. Drain juices from chicken wings into small saucepan. In a small bowl, blend cornstarch, 2 teaspoons water, sesame oil and mustard. Stir into chicken juices in saucepan. Bring to a boil. Cook, stirring constantly, until thickened. Pour over wings. Serve hot or at room temperature. Makes 8 to 12 servings.

Mexicali Party Dip

Slow oven simmering blends the flavors in this spicy dip.

2 tablespoons vegetable oil
1 medium onion, chopped
4 garlic cloves, minced
1/2 teaspoon ground cinnamon
1/2 teaspoon salt
1/4 teaspoon ground allspice
1/4 teaspoon ground cloves
1/8 teaspoon ground cumin
1/8 teaspoon red (cayenne) pepper
1 (28-oz.) can plum tomatoes, cut up

2 (4-oz.) cans diced green chilies
1 tablespoon vinegar
2 teaspoons sugar
1/4 cup raisins
1 lb. lean ground pork
1 (10-3/4-oz.) can concentrated beef broth
1 tablespoon cornstarch
1 lb. Monterey Jack cheese
Tortilla chips

In a large skillet, heat oil. Add onion and garlic; sauté 10 minutes or until tender. Turn into a shallow 1-1/2-quart casserole. Stir in cinnamon, salt, allspice, cloves, cumin, red pepper, tomatoes with juice, chilies, vinegar, sugar and raisins. Place in a cold oven. Heat oven to 350F (175C). Bake, uncovered, 1 hour, stirring 3 or 4 times. Place pork in skillet. Cook until crumbly and no longer pink; drain off fat. In a small bowl, combine beef broth and cornstarch; add to pork. Increase heat to high. Cook, stirring constantly, until mixture is thickened. Remove tomato mixture from oven. Add 1/2 of tomato mixture to pork mixture. Reserve remaining 1/2 of tomato mixture in a bowl. Shred 1/2 of cheese to give 2 cups. Slice remaining cheese. Arrange cheese slices in bottom of casserole. Top with pork mixture. Sprinkle with shredded cheese. Increase oven temperature to 400F (205C). Bake, uncovered, 8 to 10 minutes or until cheese is melted. Top with reserved tomato mixture. Bake 10 minutes longer or until tomato mixture is heated through. Serve hot with tortilla chips. Makes 15 servings.

Tip

For economy, cut apart whole chickens yourself. Freeze wings in a separate container, adding to it every time you cut up a chicken. Use the accumulated wings for a delicious party appetizer.

French Country Pâté

Offer a selection of specialty mustards with this pâté.

1-1/2 lbs. meat-loaf mix (ground veal,
    beef and pork)
8 oz. cooked ham
8 oz. pork liver or chicken livers
2 garlic cloves, minced
2 eggs
1/4 cup dry white wine
2 tablespoons Cognac

2 teaspoons salt
1 teaspoon pepper
1/2 teaspoon ground allspice
1/8 teaspoon dried leaf thyme
1/8 teaspoon crumbled bay leaf
8 oz. bacon slices
Crusty whole-grain bread

Preheat oven to 350F (175C). Place meat-loaf mix in a large bowl. Cut ham into 1/4-inch cubes. Place liver, garlic and eggs in a food processor fitted with a steel blade or blender; process until smooth. Add wine, Cognac, salt, pepper, allspice, thyme and bay leaf; process until blended. In large bowl, thoroughly combine meat-loaf mix, ham and liver mixture. Line a 1-1/2-quart crockery terrine or casserole with 1/2 of bacon slices. Spoon in liver mixture. Lay remaining bacon slices over top. Cover tightly, first with waxed paper and then with a double thickness of foil. Place in a larger pan. Pour boiling water to a depth of 1-1/2 to 2 inches in pan. Bake 1-1/2 hours or until pâté comes away from sides of dish. Baking time will vary depending on type of dish used. For example, enamelled cast iron may cook more quickly than a porous crockery. Remove terrine from oven; cover with a board or lid that fits dish. Or, cover a brick with foil and place on top of pâté. Refrigerate. To serve, cut chilled pâté into thin slices. Serve with crusty whole-grain bread. Makes about 20 slices.

Chinese Roasted Spareribs

Buy licorice-flavored star anise in Oriental markets or a spice store.

1 (2-lb.) strip pork spareribs,
    cut in half lengthwise
1/4 cup dark soy sauce
1 teaspoon sugar

3 tablespoons Chinese rice wine or sherry
3 star-anise pods
1 tablespoon hoisin sauce
2 tablespoons honey

Leave sparerib strips intact until after cooking. Place in a shallow dish. In a small bowl, combine remaining ingredients; pour over spareribs. Cover and refrigerate at least 2 hours or overnight to marinate. Baste 2 or 3 times with marinade during refrigeration. Preheat oven to 475F (245C). Place a rack in a roasting pan. Set ribs on rack, reserving marinade. Roast 20 minutes, basting once or twice with reserved marinade. Turn ribs over and reduce heat to 375F (190C). Roast 20 minutes longer or until crisp. Remove from oven. Carve strips into individual ribs. Serve hot or cold. Makes 8 servings.

How to Make French Country Pâté

1/Line a 1-1/2-quart crockery terrine with 1/2 of bacon slices.

2/Spoon liver mixture into bacon-lined terrine. Lay remaining bacon slices over top.

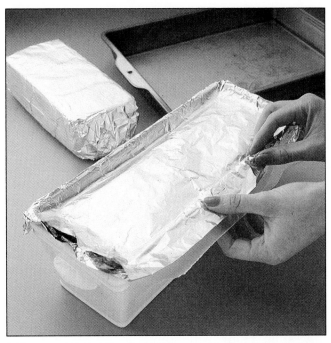

3/Cover pâté tightly, first with waxed paper, then with a double thickness of foil. Place in a larger pan with boiling water.

4/Bake until pâté comes away from sides of terrine. Place a foil-covered brick on pâté; refrigerate.

Meat

Nothing is more welcoming on a chilly day than the aroma of a casserole of beef, lamb, pork or veal, rich with herbs and vegetables, simmering unattended in the oven.

All these meat casseroles are cooked, served and stored in the same dish. Although some may be meat-stretching casseroles, many of them are simply another method of preparing cuts of meat that are not tender to start out. Casseroles allow the cook the ease of "putting it into the oven and forgetting it." Oven-simmered stews turn out succulent and tasty. Covered, the flavors stay right in the pot!

Recipes in this chapter make it easy for a host or hostess to spend a minimum of last-minute time in the kitchen, yet serve an exciting meal. All of the recipes make excellent fare for entertaining. For instance, consider Burgundy Beef, Hungarian Goulash, Italian Braised Veal Shanks or German Rouladen. Use the nationality theme as an inspiration. Carry through the theme with colors of the country, dishes, knick-knacks as center-pieces, colorful tablecloths and napkins. Often fabric stores have specials on remnants which you can use to enhance a theme. If the fabric is not wide enough to look good on the table, place a larger tablecloth of a neutral or contrasting color beneath it.

As a backdrop for the French menu, try using a blue Provençal print for the tablecloth and napkins, blue tapers for candles and tiny white wildflowers for the floral accent. Dishes in almost any solid color will complement this scheme. Red, white and green will echo the flavor of the Italian menu. Choose these colors in bold wide stripes for the tablecloth and napkins and repeat the colors for the candles. Set a little Italian flag and a cluster of small white flowers at each place setting for the final touch. White or almost any solid-color dishes will work well with this scheme.

French Country Menu

Burgundy Beef, page 39
Glazed Tiny New potatoes, Glazed Mushrooms & Glazed Carrots
Green Salad
Herb Vinaigrette
French Bread
Burgundy
Apple Streusel, page 145
Coffee

◆

Italian Country Menu

Italian Braised Veal Shanks, page 51
Hot Buttered Noodles
Salad of Romaine with Parmesan Cheese
Italian Dressing
Garlic Breadsticks
Chianti
Grapes, Cream Cheese
Espresso Coffee

Hungarian Goulash

Every Hungarian cook has a favorite recipe for goulash!

1 tablespoon butter, margarine or
  vegetable oil
1 lb. beef stew cubes
1 lb. lean pork cubes
2 medium onions, sliced
2 tablespoons sweet or hot Hungarian
  paprika

1/2 teaspoon dried leaf marjoram
1 (2-lb.) can or jar sauerkraut,
  rinsed, squeezed dry
Salt to taste
1/2 pint dairy sour cream (1 cup)
1 teaspoon caraway seeds
Hot buttered noodles

Preheat oven to 350F (175C). In a 2-1/2- to 3-quart, enamelled, cast-iron casserole or heavy Dutch oven, heat butter, margarine or oil. Add meat, a few pieces at a time, to brown thoroughly on all sides; remove pieces to a bowl or plate. When all meat is browned, add onions to skillet; sauté about 5 minutes or until wilted. Pour off excess fat. Return meat to casserole. Sprinkle with paprika and marjoram; top with sauerkraut. Bake, covered, 1 hour or until meat is tender but not dry. Add salt. To serve, stir in sour cream and caraway seeds. Serve over hot buttered noodles. Makes 6 servings.

Moroccan Beef Tajine

To eat this stew, Moroccans use chunks of anise-flavored whole-wheat bread as scoops.

2 lbs. boneless beef round,
   cut in 1-inch cubes
1-1/2 teaspoons salt
1/2 teaspoon black pepper
3 tablespoons olive oil
2 medium onions, chopped
1 teaspoon ground cumin
1/2 teaspoon ground turmeric
1/2 teaspoon ground ginger
Pinch of red (cayenne) pepper

1 (3-inch) cinnamon stick
1/2 cup chopped fresh parsley
4 tomatoes, peeled, chopped
3 tablespoons tomato paste
3/4 cup water
1 lb. fresh green beans, sliced lengthwise
   or 2 (10-oz.) pkgs. frozen French-cut
   green beans
1 tablespoon sesame seeds, toasted
Hot cooked rice

Pat meat dry with paper towels; sprinkle meat with salt and black pepper. In a 2-1/2- to 3-quart, enamelled, cast-iron casserole, heat oil. Add meat pieces, a few at a time, and brown on all sides; remove to a bowl or plate. When all meat is browned, add onions to casserole; sauté about 3 minutes or until lightly browned. Add cumin, turmeric, ginger, red pepper, cinnamon stick, parsley, tomatoes, tomato paste and water to casserole. Return meat to casserole. Bake, covered, in a 350F (175C) oven 2 hours or until meat is tender. Add more water during cooking, if necessary. Parboil fresh green beans or thaw frozen green beans. Add to casserole; bake, covered, 15 minutes longer. Remove and discard cinnamon stick. To serve, sprinkle with sesame seeds. Serve with hot cooked rice. Makes 6 servings.

Beer-Baked Irish Beef

Serve this busy-day casserole with hot soda biscuits and butter.

1/3 cup all-purpose flour
1 teaspoon salt
1 teaspoon ground allspice
1/2 teaspoon pepper
2-1/2 to 3 lbs. beef stew cubes
6 bacon slices, diced
4 carrots, cut diagonally in 1-inch lengths
4 large onions, cut in eighths

2 garlic cloves, bruised, peeled
1/4 cup minced fresh parsley
1 teaspoon dried leaf rosemary
1 teaspoon dried leaf marjoram
1 bay leaf
1 (12-oz.) can dark beer
Chopped fresh parsley
Hot buttered noodles or boiled potatoes

In a plastic bag, combine flour, salt, allspice and pepper. Place meat in bag; shake until lightly coated. In a medium, heavy skillet, cook bacon until crisp. Remove bacon and set aside, leaving drippings in skillet. Add floured beef pieces to skillet, a few at a time, and brown on all sides; remove to a deep 2-1/2-quart casserole. When all meat is browned, add carrots, onions and garlic to skillet; sauté until lightly browned. Place in casserole with meat. Drain excess fat from skillet. Sprinkle meat and vegetables with minced parsley, rosemary and marjoram; tuck bay leaf into meat mixture. Pour beer into skillet; bring to a boil, stirring constantly to scrape up meat drippings. Pour over meat mixture in casserole. Bake, covered, in a 275F (135C) oven 4 hours or until beef is very tender. Remove and discard bay leaf. Garnish with chopped parsley and cooked bacon. Serve over hot buttered noodles or with boiled potatoes. Makes 6 to 8 generous servings.

German Beef & Mushroom Bake

This is the most effortless of beef stews!

1/4 cup all-purpose flour	6 carrots, cut in 1-inch lengths
1-1/2 teaspoons salt	8 oz. fresh, small, whole mushrooms
2 lbs. beef stew cubes	10 small white onions, peeled
2 tablespoons vegetable oil or	1/2 cup chopped fresh parsley
bacon drippings	Additional chopped fresh parsley
1 (12-oz.) can beer	

Place flour and salt in a plastic bag. Place meat in bag; shake until lightly coated. In a heavy 3-quart Dutch oven, heat oil or drippings. Add floured beef pieces, a few at a time, and brown on all sides; remove to a bowl or plate. When all meat pieces are browned, return to Dutch oven. Add beer, carrots, mushrooms, onions and 1/2 cup parsley. Bake, covered, in a 325F (165C) oven 2-1/2 hours or until beef is very tender. Garnish with additional parsley. Makes 8 servings.

Swedish Meat & Potato Casserole

This is good served with pickled beets and a carrot-cabbage salad.

2 lbs. boneless beef round	1/2 teaspoon pepper
6 medium potatoes, peeled	1/2 cup water
3 tablespoons butter	1 (12-oz.) can dark beer
2 large onions, sliced	1 tablespoon Dijon-style mustard
1/2 teaspoon ground allspice	1 teaspoon cornstarch
1-1/2 teaspoons salt	1/4 cup chopped fresh parsley

Preheat oven to 375F (190C). Lightly butter a 2-1/2-quart casserole. Cut meat in 1/4-inch slices across the grain. Cut potatoes in 1/2-inch slices. To prevent browning, place potato slices in a bowl of iced water until ready to use. In a medium, heavy skillet, melt butter. Add meat slices, a few at a time, and brown on all sides; remove meat to a plate or bowl. When all meat is browned, add onions to skillet; sauté until tender. Drain potatoes; pat dry with paper towels. Layer 1/2 of potatoes in bottom of buttered casserole; sprinkle with some allspice, salt and pepper. Top with 1/2 of meat; sprinkle with more allspice, salt and pepper. Top with onions, in a single layer, then with layers of remaining meat and potatoes, sprinkling each layer with seasonings. Pour water into skillet; bring to a boil, stirring constantly to scrape up meat drippings. Cook until only 2 tablespoons liquid remain; pour over layers in casserole. Add beer to skillet; bring to a boil. Boil just until bubbles are gone. Pour over mixture in casserole. Bake, covered, 1-1/2 hours or until meat is very tender. Remove casserole from oven; pour off liquid into a small skillet. In a small bowl, blend mustard and cornstarch. Whisk into cooking liquid in skillet. Cook over medium heat until thickened and glossy, whisking constantly. Pour over meat and potatoes in casserole. Garnish with parsley. Makes 6 servings.

English Steak & Kidney Pie

This is a favorite offering in English pubs!

Mock Puff Pastry, see below
1 lb. veal or lamb kidneys
1/3 cup all-purpose flour
1-1/2 teaspoons salt
1/2 teaspoon pepper
2 teaspoons fines herbes
2 lbs. beef tenderloin tips or
    top sirloin, cut in 1-inch cubes

1/4 cup butter
1 bunch green onions, chopped,
    including tops
1 lb. fresh mushrooms, sliced
1/4 cup dry sherry
1 egg, beaten

Mock Puff Pastry:
1-1/2 cups all-purpose flour
1/2 teaspoon salt
1/2 cup plus 2 tablespoons butter, chilled

1 egg, slightly beaten
2 teaspoons lemon juice
3 to 4 tablespoons iced water

Prepare dough for Mock Puff Pastry; wrap and refrigerate. Split kidneys; remove membrane and center gristle. Cut each kidney into 2 or 3 pieces. Wash in cold water; pat dry with paper towels. In a plastic bag, combine flour, salt, pepper and herbs. Add meat and kidney pieces; shake until well-coated. Shake off excess flour. In a large skillet, melt butter. Add green onions and mushrooms; sauté 5 minutes or until onions are tender but not browned. Arrange 1/2 of meat and kidneys in a 2-1/2-quart casserole. Cover with 1/2 of mushroom mixture. Add remaining meat and kidneys; top with remaining mushroom mixture. Pour sherry evenly over top. Preheat oven to 350F (175C). On a pastry cloth or floured board, roll out chilled dough to make an 1/8-inch-thick rectangle. Roll up jelly-roll fashion and roll out again to a rectangle. Fold from long ends over the center to make a square of dough. Roll out again to fit top of casserole. Trim edges. Roll out trimmings to make decorative shapes and a long strip of dough, 3/4 inch wide, to fit around rim of casserole. Moisten inside rim of casserole. Press dough strip onto rim; moisten dough. Place rolled-out dough over filling, pressing firmly onto dough strip. Flute edge. Brush with egg. Place decorative shapes on top of dough. Using a fork, prick dough in several places to make vent holes. Brush with egg again. Bake 1 hour or until meat is tender when probed under pastry. Makes 6 to 8 servings.

Mock Puff Pastry:
In a large bowl, mix flour and salt. With a pastry blender or 2 knives, cut butter into flour until mixture is in pea-sized pieces. In a small bowl, beat egg, lemon juice and 3 tablespoons water. Sprinkle egg mixture over flour mixture; stir with a fork until dough holds together in a ball, adding more water, if necessary.

Note: Fines herbes is a combination of equal parts dried leaf thyme, oregano, marjoram, basil, rosemary and rubbed sage.

How to Make English Steak & Kidney Pie

1/Layer meat and kidneys, and mushroom mixture in a 2-1/2-quart casserole.

2/Roll out dough to fit top of casserole. Roll out trimmings to make decorative shapes and a long strip of dough to fit around rim of casserole. Moisten inside rim of casserole. Press dough strip onto rim; moisten dough.

3/Place rolled-out dough over filling, pressing firmly onto dough strip. Flute edge. Brush dough with beaten egg.

4/Place decorative shapes on top of dough. Using a fork, prick dough in several places to make vent holes. Brush with egg again. Bake until meat is tender.

Carbonnade Flamande with Dumplings

This classic beef and beer dish is from Belgium.

4 lbs. boneless lean beef round,
  cut in 1/2-inch slices
1/2 cup all-purpose flour
1/2 cup vegetable oil
2 lbs. large onions, thickly sliced
6 garlic cloves, minced
3 tablespoons brown sugar
1/4 cup red-wine vinegar
1/2 cup chopped fresh parsley

2 small bay leaves
2 teaspoons dried leaf thyme
3 teaspoons salt
Pepper to taste
4 cups beef broth
2 (12-oz.) cans dark beer
Dumplings, see below
Additional chopped fresh parsley

Dumplings:
1-1/2 cups all-purpose flour
1 tablespoon minced fresh parsley
2 teaspoons baking powder
1/2 teaspoon salt
1/8 teaspoon ground mace or ground nutmeg

2/3 cup milk
2 tablespoons butter, margarine or
  shortening, melted
1 egg, slightly beaten

Preheat oven to 325F (165C). Cut meat into 2" x 1" pieces. Place flour in a plastic bag. Place meat in bag; shake until lightly coated. In a large skillet, heat 1/2 of oil. Add floured meat pieces, a few at a time, and brown on all sides; remove to a 6-quart heatproof casserole. When all meat is browned, heat remaining oil in skillet. Add onions and garlic; sauté until browned. Add to casserole with sugar, 2 tablespoons vinegar, 1/2 cup parsley, bay leaves, thyme, salt and pepper; stir. Pour beef broth into skillet; bring to a boil, stirring constantly to scrape up meat drippings. Pour over meat mixture in casserole. Add beer. Bake, covered, 2 hours or until beef is tender. Stir in remaining vinegar. Prepare Dumplings. Place casserole on top of the range over medium-high heat. Heat until sauce bubbles. Drop dumpling batter by tablespoonfuls on top of hot stew. Cover; reduce heat and cook 15 minutes. Do not remove cover during this time. Garnish with parsley. Makes 6 to 8 servings.

Dumplings:
In a medium bowl, mix flour, parsley, baking powder, salt and mace or nutmeg. Stir in milk; butter, margarine or shortening; and egg just until dry ingredients are moistened. Drop by table-spoonfuls into hot stew as directed above. Makes 8 to 10 dumplings.

Tip

All three of these stews can be made ahead and frozen. Thaw and reheat in a 325F (165C) oven or de-frost and heat in the microwave.

Burgundy Beef   *Photo on page 129.*

This classic favorite can be made ahead and reheated.

1 lb. small white onions, peeled	1-1/2 cups water
6 bacon slices, diced	2 parsley sprigs
4 lbs. boneless beef chuck,	Leafy top from 1 celery stalk
cut in 1-1/2-inch cubes	1 carrot, quartered
1/4 cup brandy	1 bay leaf
1-1/2 teaspoons salt	1 teaspoon dried leaf thyme
1/4 teaspoon pepper	3 tablespoons cornstarch
2 cups Burgundy	1/2 cup cold water
2 garlic cloves, bruised, peeled	Chopped fresh parsley
1 lb. fresh, small, whole mushrooms	

Preheat oven to 350F (175C). In a medium, heavy skillet, brown onions and bacon; set aside. Add beef pieces to skillet, a few at a time, and brown on all sides; remove to a bowl or plate. When all meat is browned, return to skillet. In a small saucepan, warm brandy over low heat until bubbles begin to appear around edge of pan. Pour warm brandy over meat. Using a long match, carefully ignite brandy. Pour flaming brandy over meat. Stir gently until flame goes out. Place beef, bacon and onions in a deep 3-quart casserole. Sprinkle with salt and pepper. Pour some Burgundy into skillet; bring to a boil, stirring constantly to scrape up meat drippings. Pour over meat mixture in casserole. Add remaining Burgundy, garlic, mushrooms, water, parsley sprigs, celery, carrot, bay leaf and thyme to meat mixture. Bake, covered, 2 hours or until beef is very tender. Using a slotted spoon, remove beef, bacon, mushrooms and onions to a large bowl. Strain cooking liquid into skillet; discard solids. Boil cooking liquid until reduced by half. In a small bowl, blend cornstarch and water. Whisk into hot cooking liquid. Cook over medium heat until thickened, whisking constantly. Return meat, mushrooms and onions to casserole. Pour thickened cooking liquid over beef mixture. Garnish with chopped parsley. Makes 8 servings.

Finnish Three-Meat Stew

Three varieties of meat almost melt together in this long slow bake.

1 lb. beef stew cubes	2 teaspoons salt
1 lb. lamb cubes	Buttered new potatoes
1 lb. lean pork cubes	Dilled cooked carrots
5 medium onions, thinly sliced	Rye bread
1 teaspoon whole allspice	

In a deep, heavy, 2-1/2-quart casserole, layer beef, lamb and pork alternately with onions, allspice and salt. Bake, covered, in a 275F (135C) oven 5 hours or until meat is very tender. Serve with buttered new potatoes, dilled cooked carrots and rye bread. Makes 8 servings.

German Rouladen

This beef dish is often served with sweet and sour red cabbage.

1-1/4 lbs. beef top round steak,
   sliced 1/2 inch thick
4 bacon slices
Salt, pepper and minced fresh parsley
   to taste
1 large dill pickle, quartered lengthwise
All-purpose flour

2 tablespoons butter
1 cup beef broth
1/2 cup whipping cream
1 tablespoon German-style
   whole-grain mustard
Additional chopped fresh parsley

Preheat oven to 325F (165C). Cut beef into 4 square-shaped equal pieces. Place pieces between sheets of plastic wrap. Pound with the flat side of a meat mallet until thin and about tripled in size. Place a bacon slice diagonally on each piece of beef; sprinkle with salt, pepper and minced parsley. Place a piece of dill pickle on each piece of beef. Roll up tightly with pickle in center. Tie with string or secure with wooden picks. Dust lightly with flour. In a large skillet, melt butter over medium heat. Add beef rolls; cook until browned. Arrange in a single layer in a shallow 1-quart casserole. Pour broth into skillet; bring to a boil, stirring constantly to scrape up meat drippings. Pour hot broth over beef rolls in casserole. Bake, covered, 1 hour or until meat is very tender. Strain cooking juices into skillet. Bring to a boil and whisk in cream and mustard. Boil until juices are reduced to a thick sauce, about 1/3 of original amount. Pour sauce over beef rolls. Garnish with parsley. Makes 4 servings.

Variation
Use cooked carrot, sliced onion or pickled green beans in place of dill pickle, if desired.

Greek Beef with Cumin & Currants

Serve with Bulgur Baked with Raisins & Pine Nuts, page 140, and a salad.

3 lbs. boneless beef chuck,
   cut in 1-1/2-inch cubes
1 teaspoon salt
1/2 teaspoon pepper
1/4 cup butter
1 lb. small white onions, peeled
1 (8-oz.) can tomato sauce
1 tablespoon mixed pickling spices

1/2 cup dry red wine
2 tablespoons red-wine vinegar
1 garlic clove, minced
1 bay leaf, crumbled
1 (3-inch) cinnamon stick
1/2 teaspoon whole cloves
1/2 teaspoon ground cumin
1/2 cup currants or raisins

Sprinkle beef with salt and pepper. In a heavy 5- to 6-quart casserole, melt butter. Add beef; stir to coat with butter but do not brown. Add onions, tomato sauce and pickling spices. In a small bowl, combine wine, vinegar and garlic; pour over meat mixture in casserole. Add bay leaf, cinnamon stick, cloves, cumin and currants or raisins. Bake, covered, in a 300F (150C) oven 2-1/2 hours or until meat is very tender. Remove and discard cinnamon stick and other whole spices, if desired. Makes 6 servings.

Note: If the stew cooks dry and juices have separated, skim off the fat and whisk in about 1 cup broth or water to rethicken the juices.

How to Make German Rouladen

1/Cut beef into 4 square-shaped equal pieces. Place pieces between sheets of plastic wrap. Pound with the flat side of a meat mallet until thin and about tripled in size.

2/Place a bacon slice diagonally on each piece of beef; sprinkle with salt, pepper and minced parsley. Place a piece of dill pickle on each piece of beef. Roll up tightly and secure with wooden picks.

Beef & Artichoke Bake

Serve this with French Potato Gratin, page 139, and a crisp green salad.

1 (9-oz.) pkg. frozen artichoke hearts or
   1 (8-1/2-oz. net dr. wt.) can
   artichoke hearts
3 tablespoons butter
2 garlic cloves, minced
3 lbs. beef sirloin or top round steak,
   cut in 1-1/2-inch cubes

2 large onions, sliced
1/2 cup red wine
1 (8-oz.) can tomato sauce
Chopped fresh parsley

Preheat oven to 325F (165C). Cook frozen artichoke hearts according to package directions; drain and set aside. Rinse, drain and quarter canned artichoke hearts; set aside. In a medium, heavy skillet, melt butter. Add garlic and beef pieces, a few at a time, and brown on all sides; remove to a 2-quart casserole. When all meat is browned, add onions to skillet; sauté over low heat about 10 minutes or until very tender. Remove onions to casserole. Pour wine into skillet; bring to a boil, stirring constantly to scrape up meat drippings. Pour over meat mixture in casserole. Add artichokes and tomato sauce. Bake, uncovered, about 30 minutes or until beef is tender. Garnish with parsley. Makes 8 servings.

Russian Beef Pozharsky

Pozar *refers to the flaming of this dish before it is served.*

1/2 cup butter
2 medium potatoes, peeled,
   thinly sliced (about 8 oz.)
1-1/2 lbs. boneless, tender, lean beef,
   cut in 1/2-inch slices
1 large onion, sliced
4 oz. fresh mushrooms, sliced
1 large tomato, peeled
1-1/2 tablespoons all-purpose flour

1 cup beef broth
1/2 cup dry white wine
1 tablespoon tomato paste
1 tablespoon lemon juice
1/4 teaspoon salt
1/4 teaspoon dried leaf basil
1/4 teaspoon dry mustard
Pepper to taste
3 tablespoons brandy

In a large skillet, melt 2 tablespoons butter over medium heat. Add potatoes; cook, lifting and turning them, just until tender and slightly browned. Arrange potatoes over bottom of a shallow 1-1/2-quart casserole. In skillet, melt 2 tablespoons butter. Add meat; brown quickly on all sides over high heat. Remove to casserole. In same skillet, melt 1 tablespoon butter. Add onion; sauté until tender. Spoon over meat. In same skillet, melt 2 tablespoons butter. Add mushrooms; sauté about 3 minutes or until browned. Spoon mushrooms over onion. Slice tomato into 4 thick slices; place on top of mushrooms. Preheat oven to 350F (175C). In skillet, melt remaining butter. Stir in flour until smooth. Whisk in beef broth and wine; bring to a boil, whisking constantly until thickened and smooth. Stir in tomato paste, lemon juice, salt, basil, mustard and pepper. Spoon over meat mixture in casserole. Bake, covered, 40 minutes or until meat is tender. Just before serving, warm brandy in a small saucepan over low heat until bubbles begin to appear around edge of pan. Using a long match, carefully ignite brandy. Pour flaming brandy over meat. Let flames die out without stirring. Makes 6 servings.

Short Ribs & Onions

When you prebrown ribs in the oven, it saves dishwashing!

1/3 cup all-purpose flour
1 teaspoon salt
1 teaspoon paprika
3 lbs. beef short ribs,
   cut in 2-1/2-inch pieces

2 cups hot beef broth
2 large onions, sliced
4 to 6 servings hot cooked noodles
Chopped fresh parsley

Preheat oven to 450F (230C). Line a 15" x 10" jelly-roll pan with foil. In a small bowl, mix flour, salt and paprika; coat short ribs with flour mixture. Place ribs well apart on prepared pan. Bake, uncovered, 20 minutes, turning 3 times to brown on all sides. Remove from oven and reduce temperature to 325F (165C). Transfer ribs to a 2-quart casserole. Pour hot broth over ribs; top with onions. Bake, covered, 1-1/2 to 2 hours or until meat is very tender. Remove ribs to a warm serving platter. Add cooked noodles to hot juices in casserole; gently stir. Garnish with parsley. Serve ribs with juice-flavored noodles. Makes 4 to 6 servings.

Irish Lamb Casserole

This extra-easy casserole is best made a day ahead.

12 medium, red-skinned potatoes, peeled
4 large onions, quartered
3 lbs. lamb cubes
8 oz. thick-sliced lean bacon,
　cut in 1/2-inch pieces
1 teaspoon dried leaf thyme

3 tablespoons minced fresh parsley
2 teaspoons salt
1 teaspoon pepper
3 cups beef broth or lamb broth
1 bay leaf

Preheat oven to 350F (175C). Slice 1/2 of potatoes; layer in bottom of a deep 3-quart Dutch oven or casserole. Slice onions 1/2 inch thick; layer 1/2 of onions over potatoes. Arange lamb and bacon over onions; sprinkle with thyme, parsley, 1/2 teaspoon salt and 1/2 teaspoon pepper. Cover with remaining onions. Arrange remaining whole potatoes over onions; pour broth over potato mixture. Sprinkle with remaining salt and pepper; tuck bay leaf into mixture. Bake, covered, 2-1/2 hours or until meat is very tender and bottom potatoes have cooked down to make a sauce. If made a day ahead, cover and refrigerate. Skim any fat from top and reheat, covered, in a 350F (175C) oven about 30 minutes or until heated through. Remove and discard bay leaf. Makes 6 servings.

Bulgarian Lamb Moussaka

This is a wonderfully simple, tasty and economical party dish!

4 (12-oz.) eggplants, peeled,
　cut in 1/2-inch slices
Salt
2 tablespoons butter
1 large onion, chopped
2 lbs. lean ground lamb
2 teaspoons salt
1 teaspoon paprika

Pepper to taste
1 teaspoon dried leaf oregano
Olive oil
4 tomatoes, peeled, sliced
1/2 pint plain yogurt (1 cup)
4 egg yolks
1/2 cup all-purpose flour

Sprinkle eggplant slices lightly with salt. Place on a double layer of paper towels; let stand 1 hour to release bitter liquid. In a large heavy skillet, melt butter. Add onion; sauté 10 minutes over low heat. Add meat, 2 teaspoons salt, paprika, pepper and oregano. Cook and stir 5 to 10 minutes or until meat is crumbly and no longer pink. Preheat broiler. Pat eggplant slices dry with paper towels. Sprinkle eggplant slices with olive oil. Broil about 3 inches from heat until lightly browned on 1 side; turn and broil on the other side. Preheat oven to 350F (175C). Butter a shallow 3-quart casserole or 13" x 9" baking dish. Arrange alternate layers of meat mixture and eggplant in buttered casserole. Top with tomato slices in casserole. Bake, uncovered, 1 hour. In a small bowl, blend yogurt, egg yolks and flour. Pour over tomato layer in casserole. Bake, uncovered, 15 minutes longer or until custard is golden. Let stand 15 minutes before serving. Makes 6 to 8 servings.

Shown on following pages: Lamb Curry, page 46.

Lamb Curry   *Photo on pages 44 and 45.*

A fresh-fruit salad makes a refreshing dessert after curry.

4 lbs. boneless lamb shoulder,
    cut in 1-inch cubes
1 cup golden raisins
1 cup shredded coconut
2 cups water
5 tablespoons vegetable oil
1 cup coarsely chopped onion
5 large garlic cloves, chopped
1-1/4 cups chicken broth
2/3 cup mango chutney
1/4 cup Indian curry powder

2 tablespoons coriander seeds
1/4 teaspoon ground mace
1/4 teaspoon ground cloves
1/4 teaspoon ground cinnamon
1 teaspoon salt
Pinch of red (cayenne) pepper, if desired
2 tablespoons cornstarch
2 tablespoons cold water
Sambals, see below
4 cups hot cooked rice

Sambals:

1 cup Indian, mango, or homemade chutney
1 cup finely chopped peanuts
1 cup finely chopped red onion
1 cup finely chopped green-onion tops
1 cup finely chopped cucumber
1 cup finely chopped tomato, drained
1 medium, green bell pepper,
    cut in 1-inch strips
1 cup finely chopped canned beets

1 cup bite-sized banana pieces,
    sprinkled with lemon juice
1 cup bite-sized apple pieces,
    sprinkled with lemon juice
1 cup drained pineapple tidbits or chunks
1 cup drained mandarin-orange segments
1 cup finely chopped hard-cooked egg
1 cup crumbled crisp-cooked bacon

Pat lamb dry with paper towels. In 2 small bowls, soak raisins and coconut each in 1 cup water 1 hour. Drain raisins and coconut, reserving liquids; set raisins aside. Pat coconut dry with paper towels. In a small skillet, heat 1 tablespoon oil over medium heat. Add coconut; toss until golden brown. Set aside. In a large heavy skillet, heat 3 tablespoons oil. Add lamb, a few pieces at a time, and brown on all sides; remove to a 3-quart Dutch oven. When all lamb is browned, reduce heat to low. In skillet, heat remaining 1 tablespoon oil. Add onion; sauté 5 minutes. Add garlic; sauté 3 minutes longer. Remove from heat. Stir in chicken broth, chutney, curry powder, coriander, mace, cloves, cinnamon, salt and red pepper, if desired. Add reserved soaking liquid from raisins and coconut; bring to a boil. Pour over lamb in Dutch oven. Bake, covered, in a 300F (150C) oven 2 hours or until meat is tender. Prepare at least 8 Sambals of your choice, including soaked raisins and toasted coconut. Remove curry from oven. In a small bowl, blend cornstarch and water. Bring curry to a boil over high heat. Add cornstarch mixture; cook and stir about 2 minutes or until thickened. Serve with hot cooked rice and Sambals. Makes 10 to 12 servings.

Sambals are an assortment of condiments traditionally served with curry-type dishes in Southeast Asia.

Wine-Braised Lamb Shanks

Bake Easy Rice & Tomato Pilaf, page 138, along with this richly flavored meat.

4 (1-lb.) lamb shanks
1/4 cup all-purpose flour
1 teaspoon salt
1/2 teaspoon pepper
2 tablespoons olive oil or vegetable oil

2 cups red wine
1 garlic clove, minced
1 teaspoon dried leaf basil
1 teaspoon dried leaf oregano

Ask the butcher to crack the lamb shanks. In a small bowl, mix flour, salt and pepper; coat lamb with flour mixture. In a 2-1/2-quart, enamelled, cast-iron casserole, heat oil. Add floured lamb shanks; quickly brown on all sides. Add wine, garlic, basil and oregano. Bake, covered, in a 350F (175C) oven 2 hours or until meat is tender. Spoon pan drippings over meat to serve. Makes 4 servings.

Pork & Eggplant Casserole

Serve this casserole with a whole-grain peasant bread and salad.

1 lb. lean pork cubes
3 potatoes, peeled, cut in 1-inch cubes
1 large eggplant, peeled,
    cut in 1-inch cubes
1 large onion, coarsely chopped
3 tomatoes, peeled, diced
2 leeks, chopped

1/2 cup chopped fresh parsley
2 cups dry white wine or water
2 teaspoons salt
1/2 teaspoon pepper
1 cup shredded, mild, white cheese,
    such as white Cheddar or
    Monterey Jack (4 oz.)

Preheat oven to 375F (190C). Butter a 2-1/2-quart casserole. In a large bowl, combine all ingredients except cheese; turn into buttered casserole. Bake, covered, 1-1/2 hours or until meat and vegetables are tender. Remove cover and sprinkle with cheese. Bake, uncovered, 15 minutes longer or until cheese is melted. Makes 6 to 8 servings.

Freeze cooled leftover casserole mixture in single-serving quantities in heavy-duty zip-top plastic bags. Label and stack flat in the freezer.

Pork-Chop & Apple Bake

Perfect for chilly autumn days, served with dark rye bread.

1/4 cup all-purpose flour
1/2 teaspoon salt
1/2 teaspoon dry mustard
1/8 teaspoon pepper
1/8 teaspoon ground allspice
4 (1-inch-thick) pork chops
2 tablespoons butter

2 tablespoons brown sugar
1-1/2 cups apple cider
2 apples, cored, peeled, sliced
1/3 cup raisins
1/2 teaspoon ground cinnamon
Caraway Buttered Noodles, see below

Caraway Buttered Noodles:
1 (8-oz.) pkg. egg noodles
1/4 cup butter

1 teaspoon caraway seeds

Lightly butter a shallow 2-quart casserole or 8-inch-square baking dish. In a small bowl, mix flour, salt, mustard, pepper and allspice. Dredge pork chops with flour mixture, reserving extra flour mixture. In a large skillet, melt butter. Add floured pork chops; brown on both sides. Place chops in buttered casserole. Preheat oven to 350F (175C). Stir brown sugar and 2 tablespoons reserved flour mixture into meat drippings in skillet to make a thick paste. Gradually whisk in cider; bring to a boil, whisking constantly until thickened and smooth. Arrange apple slices over chops in casserole; sprinkle with raisins and pour sauce over all. Sprinkle with cinnamon. Bake, covered, 1 hour or until chops are tender. Prepare Caraway Buttered Noodles; serve immediately with chops. Makes 4 servings.

Caraway Buttered Noodles:
Cook noodles according to package directions until tender but firm to the bite; drain well. In a small skillet, heat butter with caraway seeds until butter melts. Turn noodles into a warm serving dish; drizzle with butter mixture. Toss to coat evenly.

Oven-Barbecued Country-Style Ribs

This is the easiest way to prepare juicy barbecued ribs!

3 lbs. country-style pork spareribs or
  pork back ribs
2 teaspoons salt
1/2 teaspoon pepper
1 large onion, chopped
1/4 cup cider vinegar
1/4 cup packed brown sugar

1 cup ketchup
3 tablespoons lemon juice
1 tablespoon prepared mustard
Few drops hot-pepper sauce
Few drops liquid-smoke flavoring,
  if desired
1/2 cup water

Preheat oven to 325F (165C). In a large heavy skillet, slowly brown ribs over medium heat, pushing them around skillet to keep them from sticking. Sprinkle with salt and pepper on both sides; remove to a shallow 3-quart casserole or 13" x 9" baking dish. Pour off all but 2 tablespoons fat from skillet. Add onion to skillet; sauté 5 minutes or until tender. Add remaining ingredients and bring to a boil, stirring constantly. Cook until sauce is slightly thickened and the consistency of ketchup. Spoon over ribs in casserole. Bake, uncovered, 1-1/2 hours or until ribs are tender, basting 2 or 3 times. Serve directly from casserole. Makes 6 servings.

How to Make Pork-Chop & Apple Bake

1/Arrange apple slices over chops in casserole; sprinkle with raisins and pour sauce over all. Sprinkle with cinnamon.

2/Bake chops until tender. Serve with Caraway Buttered Noodles.

Sweet & Sour Country-Style Ribs

Country-style ribs are cut from the pork loin.

1 teaspoon salt
3 lbs. country-style pork spareribs or
   pork back ribs
1/4 cup dark soy sauce
1/4 cup sherry
1/4 cup packed brown sugar
1/3 cup cider vinegar
2 teaspoons grated fresh gingerroot or
   1/2 teaspoon ground ginger
1/2 cup water or juice from canned pineapple

1 to 2 teaspoons Szechwan peppers or
   1 dried hot chili, crumbled
1 green bell pepper, diced
1 (8-oz.) can whole water chestnuts,
   drained
1 (8-oz.) can pineapple chunks, drained
2 teaspoons cornstarch
2 teaspoons cold water
1/2 teaspoon sesame oil
Hot cooked rice

Preheat oven to 350F (175C). Sprinkle salt in a large heavy skillet. Add spareribs; brown on all sides over medium heat. Remove to a shallow 3-quart casserole or 13" x 9" baking dish. Add soy sauce, sherry, sugar, vinegar, ginger, 1/2 cup water or pineapple juice, and Szechwan or chili pepper to skillet in which pork was browned. Bring to a boil, stirring constantly to scrape up meat drippings. Pour mixture over pork in casserole. Bake, covered, 1 hour. Add green pepper, water chestnuts and pineapple to mixture in casserole. Bake, covered, 30 minutes longer. Drain juices from casserole into a small saucepan. In a small bowl, blend cornstarch, 2 teaspoons cold water and sesame oil. Stir into meat juices. Bring to a boil; cook, stirring constantly, 1 to 2 minutes or until thickened. Pour over meat in casserole. Bake, uncovered, 15 minutes longer or until meat is tender and juices are clear and thickened. Serve over hot cooked rice. Makes 6 servings.

Old-World Sausage & Cabbage Casserole

Serve with fresh brown bread, steamed beans and an apple dessert.

4 oz. bacon slices, diced
1 medium onion, chopped
2 garlic cloves, minced
8 oz. smoked Polish sausage,
   cut in 1-inch pieces
4 oz. cooked ham, cut in 1/2-inch cubes
1 lb. lean ground pork
2 tablespoons sweet Hungarian paprika
2 teaspoons crushed caraway seeds

2 large red-skinned potatoes, scrubbed,
   cut in 1/4-inch slices
1 small cabbage, shredded (about 6 cups)
1 (2-lb.) can or jar sauerkraut,
   rinsed, squeezed dry
1 pint dairy sour cream (2 cups)
Pepper to taste
Additional paprika

Preheat oven to 350F (175C). Butter a deep 3- to 4-quart casserole. In a large heavy skillet, cook bacon over medium heat about 5 minutes or until browned. Add onion and garlic; sauté 3 to 4 minutes or until tender but not browned. Add sausage, ham and pork; cook, stirring occasionally, until meat is no longer pink. Remove from heat; drain off fat. Return skillet to heat. Add 2 tablespoons paprika and caraway seeds. Cook 2 minutes longer and remove from heat. Arrange 1/2 of potatoes in a layer in buttered casserole. Top with 1/2 of shredded cabbage and 1/2 of sauerkraut, then add meat mixture. Top with 1/2 cup sour cream. Add remaining potato slices, cabbage and sauerkraut. Spread top with remaining sour cream; sprinkle generously with pepper and additional paprika. Bake, uncovered, 1 hour or until browned around edges. Cool 15 minutes before serving. Makes 6 servings.

Quick Cassoulet

This recipe cuts hours of preparation from the original!

2 lbs. fresh garlic sausage or
   Polish sausage
2 cups chopped onion
2 cups dry white vermouth
2 cups sliced carrot
1 tablespoon sugar
1 (16-oz.) can red kidney beans, drained
1 (16-oz.) can white beans, drained

1 (16-oz.) can stewed tomatoes
9 garlic cloves, minced
5 bay leaves
2 tablespoons chopped fresh parsley
1 tablespoon dried leaf thyme
1 teaspoon ground allspice
4 bacon slices

Preheat oven to 350F (175C). Place sausage in a large heavy skillet. Brown slowly over medium heat about 10 minutes. Add onion and vermouth; simmer until vermouth has evaporated, turning sausage several times. While sausage simmers, place carrot, 2 cups water and sugar in a medium saucepan. Bring to a boil; simmer until carrot is tender. Drain. Place sausage and onion in a 2-quart casserole. Top with cooked carrot, beans, tomatoes with juice, garlic, bay leaves, parsley, thyme and allspice. Lay bacon slices over top. Bake, covered, 45 minutes or until bacon is browned and juices bubble. Remove and discard bay leaves. Makes 6 servings.

Italian Braised Veal Shanks

Italians call this Osso Bucco *which translates as* hollow bone.

1/4 cup all-purpose flour
1/2 teaspoon salt
1/4 teaspoon pepper
4 veal shanks, 2 inches thick
1/4 cup olive oil or vegetable oil
1 medium onion, quartered
1 medium carrot, cut in chunks
1 celery stalk, cut in 2-inch pieces

1 whole garlic clove, bruised, peeled
1/2 cup dry white wine
1/2 cup beef broth
1 (28-oz.) can Italian plum tomatoes
1/2 teaspoon dried leaf basil
1/2 teaspoon dried leaf rosemary
1/2 teaspoon dried leaf marjoram
Gremolata, see below

Gremolata:
6 garlic cloves, minced
2 tablespoons grated lemon peel

1/2 cup minced fresh parsley

Preheat oven to 325F (165C). In a small bowl, mix flour, salt and pepper; coat veal with flour mixture. In a large heavy skillet, heat 1/2 of oil. Add veal, a few pieces at a time, and cook until browned and crusty; remove to a large plate. In another large skillet, heat remaining oil. Add onion, carrot, celery and garlic; sauté until tender. Place onion mixture in a 3-quart casserole. Arrange veal on top of vegetables. Pour wine into skillet used for browning veal and bring to a boil, stirring constantly to scrape up meat drippings. Add broth, tomatoes with juice, and herbs; bring to a boil. Pour tomato mixture over veal mixture in casserole. Bake, covered, 2-1/2 hours or until veal is very tender. While veal cooks, prepare Gremolata. Drain juices from casserole into a medium skillet. Bring to a boil and boil hard until juices are thickened and reduced to 1-1/2 cups. Serve with Gremolata to sprinkle over veal. Makes 3 to 4 servings.

Gremolata:
In a small bowl, mix garlic, lemon peel and parsley. Turn into a serving bowl. Makes 1/2 cup.

Ham, Cabbage & Noodle Casserole

This is even better when prepared a day ahead and reheated!

1/2 medium cabbage
1 (8-oz.) pkg. egg noodles
3 cups milk
1/4 cup butter

3 cups ground cooked ham
3 eggs, beaten
1/2 teaspoon caraway seeds

Butter a 3-quart casserole. Shred cabbage in 2-inch pieces; set aside. Cook noodles according to package directions until tender but firm to the bite; drain. Rinse with cold water to prevent sticking; drain well. Preheat oven to 350F (175C). In a medium saucepan, heat milk until bubbles form around edge of pan. Remove from heat; set aside. In a large heavy skillet, melt butter. Add cabbage in batches; sauté over medium-high heat 5 minutes or until tender. Layer 1/2 of cooked noodles in buttered casserole; add 1/2 of sautéed cabbage in an even layer, then add ham in an even layer. Top with remaining cabbage, then remaining noodles. In a medium bowl, beat scalded milk and eggs; add caraway seeds. Pour over cabbage mixture in casserole. Bake, uncovered, 1 hour or until a knife inserted in center comes out clean. Makes 8 servings.

Poultry

Time was when chicken and turkey were both expensive meats and were reserved for special occasions. Recipes were aimed at extending the yields, and there was even a dish known as *Mock Chicken Legs* made of veal!

Today, chicken and turkey are not only economical, they fit in well with our calorie-conscious eating. In fact, we use them so much that the challenge is to find new and creative ways to serve them. Both chicken and turkey are featured frequently in international cooking, so we have a world of choice in planning menus.

You can choose international themes for menus by following the suggestion of the casserole itself. You'll find a rich variety from sumptuously sauced and seasoned chicken to one-dish meals which include a starch and a vegetable. Boneless chicken breasts in a casserole make an elegant company dish.

The most economical way to buy chicken is whole. Save money by cutting it up yourself. Once you have done that, it is easy to go on and bone the breasts. When you cut up a chicken yourself, you have the added bonus of trimmings which make an excellent broth when simmered with celery, carrot and onion in water to cover.

It is best to cook boneless chicken breasts on their own and not mixed in with other chicken parts because the breasts cook faster than legs and thighs. Legs, thighs and wings can be used in any recipe that calls for a whole cut-up chicken. You can always add extra legs and thighs to make up for the missing breast pieces.

While whole turkey is the all-time holiday favorite, I sometimes cook it just to have the meat for some of my favorite casseroles. The recipes here will serve well the day after a holiday and throughout the year!

> ## Anniversary Dinner
> Baked Mushrooms with Cheese, page 26
> Crab-Stuffed Turkey Breasts, page 66
> Salad of Edible Pea Pods, Bean Sprouts & Fresh Mushrooms
> Herb Vinaigrette
> Fresh-Fruit Platter
> Chocolates
> Coffee
>
> ◆
>
> ## Dinner Party for Good Friends
> Brie, Crackers, Chablis
> Chicken, Artichoke & Mushroom Bake, page 59
> Salad of Romaine, Boston & Leaf Lettuce
> Herb Vinaigrette
> Crusty French Bread, Unsalted Butter
> German-Chocolate Soufflé, page 154
> Coffee

Cheese-Stuffed Chicken Breasts

For economy, bone the chicken breasts yourself.

8 chicken-breast halves, skinned, boned
1/2 teaspoon seasoned salt
1/2 cup butter, room temperature
1/2 teaspoon dried leaf oregano, crushed
1/2 teaspoon chopped fresh parsley

4 oz. Havarti or Monterey Jack cheese, cut in 8 slices
1/2 cup seasoned breadcrumbs
1/2 cup dry white wine
Avocado slices
Tomato wedges

Preheat oven to 375F (190C). Wash chicken breasts; pat dry with paper towels. Place chicken-breast pieces between sheets of plastic wrap. Pound with the flat side of a meat mallet until thin and about doubled in size. Sprinkle seasoned salt over chicken. In a small bowl, combine butter, oregano and parsley. Spread 1/2 of butter mixture over 1 side of chicken breasts. Top each with a slice of cheese. Roll up each chicken breast tightly, tucking in ends to make each stuffed breast the same length as the others. Place in a shallow 1-1/2-quart casserole. In a small saucepan, melt remaining butter mixture; brush over chicken rolls. Sprinkle with breadcrumbs. Add wine to casserole. Bake, uncovered, 30 to 40 minutes or until tender and browned. Be careful not to over-cook chicken breasts. Garnish with avocado slices and tomato wedges. Makes 4 to 8 servings.

Cashew Chicken

This favorite dish is simple to prepare at home.

5 dried black Chinese mushrooms
Warm water
2 to 3 tablespoons vegetable oil
1 large onion, halved,
   thinly sliced lengthwise
4 chicken-breast halves, skinned, boned
1 tablespoon light soy sauce
3 tablespoons sweet sherry
3 tablespoons oyster sauce
1/4 teaspoon sugar
1/4 teaspoon white pepper
2 whole garlic cloves, bruised, peeled

1 (1/8-inch-thick) slice fresh gingerroot,
   flattened
2 teaspoons cornstarch
2 teaspoons cold water
5 water chestnuts, sliced
1/2 cup cashews, preferably unsalted
4 oz. fresh edible pea pods, trimmed, or
   1 (6-oz.) pkg. thawed frozen pea pods,
   drained
1/2 teaspoon sesame oil
Hot cooked rice

In a small bowl, cover mushrooms with warm water; soak 1 hour. Drain, reserving 1/2 cup soaking liquid; squeeze out excesss water from mushrooms. Cut off and discard stems; cut mushroom caps into quarters. Set aside. Preheat oven to 375F (190C). In a large skillet or wok, heat 1 tablespoon vegetable oil. Add onion; sauté quickly over medium-high heat until translucent. Arrange onion over bottom of a 3-quart casserole. Wash chicken breasts; pat dry with paper towels. Cut chicken, crosswise, in 1-inch slices. Add remaining vegetable oil to skillet. Add chicken; sauté quickly until browned. Arrange chicken in casserole over onion. Add soy sauce, sherry, oyster sauce, sugar, white pepper, garlic, gingerroot and reserved mushroom liquid to skillet. In a small bowl, blend cornstarch and cold water. Stir into sherry mixture in skillet. Heat to a simmer; cook, stirring constantly, until thickened. Pour over chicken mixture in casserole; add mushrooms. Bake, covered, 35 minutes or until bubbly and chicken is tender. Add water chestnuts, cashews and pea pods. Cover and return to oven 5 minutes. Discard gingerroot. Drizzle with sesame oil. Remove and discard whole garlic cloves. Serve with hot cooked rice. Makes 4 servings.

Senegalese Chicken with Peanuts

Peanuts are an important crop in the West African country of Senegal.

1 (3-lb.) chicken, cut up, or
   3 lbs. chicken legs and thighs
1/2 cup peanut oil
2 medium onions, chopped
2 cups chicken broth, heated to simmering
1/2 cup crunchy peanut butter

1 (6-oz.) can tomato paste
Salt and black pepper to taste
Red (cayenne) pepper
Hot cooked rice
Chopped hard-cooked eggs
Chopped peanuts

Preheat oven to 350F (175C). Wash chicken; pat dry with paper towels. Cut apart legs and thighs. In a 3-quart, enamelled, cast-iron casserole, heat oil. Add chicken pieces, a few at a time, and brown on both sides. Add onions; reduce heat to low. In a medium bowl, blend chicken broth, peanut butter and tomato paste; pour over chicken. Sprinkle with salt, black pepper and red pepper. Bake, covered, 45 minutes to 1 hour or until chicken is tender. Serve over hot cooked rice. Garnish with hard-cooked eggs and peanuts. Makes 4 servings.

Cashew Chicken, above, with Curried Rice & Carrots, page 138.

Chinese Potted Chicken

Serve curry condiments, page 46, to add to the Eastern flair of this dish.

1 (3- to 3-1/2-lb.) chicken, cut up, or
  3 to 3-1/2 lbs. chicken legs and thighs
3 tablespoons peanut oil
1 drop sesame oil
1 (8-oz.) can sliced water chestnuts,
  drained
1 (8-oz.) can bamboo shoots, drained
2 green onions, thinly sliced
1 teaspoon shredded fresh gingerroot

4 oz. fresh mushrooms, sliced
1-1/2 cups sliced celery
5 cups water
1 tablespoon cornstarch
3 tablespoons soy sauce
3 tablespoons sherry
1 teaspoon sugar
Hot cooked rice or thin Chinese noodles

Preheat oven to 350F (175C). Wash chicken pieces; pat dry with paper towels. Cut apart legs and thighs. In a large skillet, heat peanut and sesame oils. Add chicken pieces, a few at a time, and brown on both sides; remove to a heavy 2-quart casserole. When all chicken is browned, combine water chestnuts, bamboo shoots, green onions, gingerroot, mushrooms, celery and water in same skillet. Bring to a boil; boil 3 minutes. Spoon over chicken in casserole. Bake, covered, 1 hour or until chicken is tender. In a small bowl, blend cornstarch, soy sauce, sherry and sugar. Stir into juices in casserole. Bake, uncovered, 10 to 15 minutes or until juices are thickened. Serve over hot cooked rice or thin Chinese noodles. Makes 4 to 6 servings.

Chicken with Wild Rice & Raisins

A green salad, sprinkled with sunflower kernels, makes a great accompaniment to this dish.

1 cup uncooked wild rice or
  wild rice mixed with white rice
2-1/2 cups water
1/2 cup golden raisins
1/2 cup orange juice
6 chicken-breast halves or
  1 (3-lb.) chicken, cut up
1/4 cup all-purpose flour

1 teaspoon dried leaf tarragon
1/2 teaspoon paprika
1 teaspoon salt
1/8 teaspoon white pepper
2 tablespoons butter
2 tablespoons vegetable oil
1/2 pint whipping cream (1 cup)
1/2 cup milk

Lightly butter a shallow 2-quart casserole. Rinse wild rice in 3 changes of hot tap water or until water is no longer cloudy. Place rice and water in a medium saucepan; cover. Simmer 45 minutes or until rice is tender and has absorbed all the liquid. In a small saucepan, combine raisins and orange juice. Bring to a boil; reduce heat and simmer 5 minutes. Wash chicken; pat dry with paper towels. If using a whole chicken, cut apart legs and thighs. On a large plate, mix flour, tarragon, paprika, salt and white pepper. Roll chicken in flour mixture until coated. Reserve remaining flour mixture. In a large heavy skillet, heat butter and oil. Add chicken pieces; brown quickly over medium-high heat. Remove chicken pieces; set aside. Stir reserved flour mixture into drippings in skillet. Stir in cream and milk; bring to a boil, stirring constantly. Boil 1 minute. Add raisin-orange mixture. Preheat oven to 350F (175C). Arrange rice in buttered casserole. Cover with 1/2 of sauce. Top with chicken and remaining sauce. Bake, uncovered, about 30 minutes or until bubbly and chicken is tender. Makes 6 servings.

Chicken & Broccoli Supreme

To save time, cook chicken, broccoli and sauces a day ahead.

6 chicken-breast halves
2 cups water
2 teaspoons salt
Few celery leaves
1 medium onion, quartered
2 lbs. fresh broccoli

White Sauce, see below
Tarragon Hollandaise, see below
1/2 cup whipping cream, whipped
1 cup grated Parmesan cheese (3 oz.)
Avocado slices

White Sauce:
3 tablespoons butter
3 tablespoons all-purpose flour
1 cup liquid from cooking chicken

1 cup milk
3 tablespoons dry sherry
Salt and pepper to taste

Tarragon Hollandaise:
2 egg yolks
2 tablespoons lemon juice
1/2 cup butter, melted

1 teaspoon dried leaf tarragon
1/2 teaspoon salt

Preheat oven to 400F (205C). Butter a shallow 2-1/2- to 3-quart casserole. Wash chicken breasts; pat dry with paper towels. Place chicken breasts, water, salt, celery leaves and onion in a large saucepan. Bring to a boil. Reduce heat to low; simmer 25 minutes or until chicken is tender. Cool. Strain chicken cooking liquid, reserving 1 cup to use in White Sauce. Remove and discard skin and bones from chicken; shred meat into 2-inch lengths. Set aside. Remove flowerets from broccoli. Cut off and discard tough ends from broccoli stalks. Peel remaining stalks if skin is tough; shred stalks. In a medium saucepan, cook flowerets in boiling salted water about 10 minutes or until crisp-tender; drain and set aside. In same saucepan, combine shredded broccoli stalks and 1/4 cup water. Cover and steam 5 minutes; drain. Arrange flowerets and stalks over bottom of buttered casserole. Prepare White Sauce and Tarragon Hollandaise. In a medium bowl, combine sauces; fold in whipped cream. Sprinkle 1/2 of Parmesan cheese over broccoli in casserole. Arrange chicken over top. Spoon sauce mixture over chicken; sprinkle with remaining Parmesan cheese. Bake, uncovered, 20 minutes or until heated through and sauce is bubbly. Preheat broiler; broil 5 inches from heat until lightly browned. Garnish with avocado slices. Makes 6 to 8 servings.

White Sauce:
In a medium saucepan, melt butter. Stir in flour until smooth. Whisk in 1 cup liquid from cooking chicken, and milk; bring to a boil, whisking constantly until thickened and smooth. Stir in sherry; simmer 2 minutes, stirring constantly. Add salt and pepper. Makes 2 cups.

Tarragon Hollandaise:
In a small metal bowl, whisk together egg yolks and lemon juice. Place over a shallow pan of boiling water; do not let bowl touch water. Slowly whisk in melted butter until sauce is thick. Whisk in tarragon and salt. Makes 1/2 cup.

Jalapeño Chicken Legs

The topping on this baked chicken is creamy, yet spicy.

6 chicken legs with thighs attached
2 tablespoons vegetable oil
1 pint dairy sour cream (2 cups)
1 teaspoon salt
1/2 teaspoon black pepper

2 tablespoons all-purpose flour
1 garlic clove, minced
1 to 2 canned whole jalapeño peppers
1 large onion, sliced
1 (4-oz.) can diced green chilies

Preheat oven to 350F (175C). Wash chicken; pat dry with paper towels. In a large heavy skillet, heat oil. Add chicken pieces, a few at a time, and brown on both sides. In a food processor fitted with a steel blade or blender, combine sour cream, salt, black pepper, flour, garlic and jalapeño peppers; process until smooth. Arrange browned chicken in a shallow 3-quart casserole or 13" x 9" baking dish. Pour sour-cream mixture over chicken. Top with onion and green chilies. Bake, uncovered, 40 minutes or until chicken is tender. Makes 6 servings.

Oven-Barbecued Chicken

This is the easiest way to make barbecued chicken!

Old-Fashioned Barbecue Sauce, see below
1 (2-1/2- to 3-lb.) chicken, cut up, or
  2-1/2 to 3 lbs. chicken legs and thighs
1/2 cup all-purpose flour

1 teaspoon salt
1/8 teaspoon red (cayenne) pepper
1/4 cup butter
1/4 cup vegetable oil

Old-Fashioned Barbecue Sauce:
1 tablespoon vegetable oil
1/2 cup sliced onion
1/2 cup chopped celery
1/2 cup diced green bell pepper
1 cup ketchup

1 cup water
2 tablespoons Worcestershire sauce
2 tablespoons brown sugar
1/8 teaspoon black pepper

Preheat oven to 325F (165C). Prepare Old-Fashioned Barbecue Sauce; set aside. Wash chicken; pat dry with paper towels. Cut apart legs and thighs. In a small bowl, mix flour, salt and red pepper; coat chicken pieces with flour mixture. In a large skillet, heat butter and oil. Add floured chicken pieces, a few at a time, and brown on both sides; remove to a shallow 2-1/2- to 3-quart casserole or 13" x 9" baking dish. Pour barbecue sauce evenly over chicken. Bake, uncovered, 45 to 50 minutes or until chicken is tender. Makes 4 servings.

Old-Fashioned Barbecue Sauce:
In a medium skillet, heat oil. Add onion; sauté about 5 minutes or until tender. Stir in remaining ingredients; simmer 15 minutes. Makes about 2-1/2 cups.

How to Make Jalapeño Chicken Legs

1/Brown chicken legs, a few at a time, in hot oil.

2/Pour sour-cream mixture over chicken. Top with onion and green chilies. Bake until chicken is tender.

Chicken, Artichoke & Mushroom Bake

A sliced-orange salad makes a refreshing side dish for this casserole.

1 (9-oz.) pkg. frozen artichoke hearts or
  1 (8-1/2-oz. net dr. wt.) can
  artichoke hearts
1 (3-lb.) chicken, cut up, or
  3 lbs. chicken legs and thighs
1-1/2 teaspoons salt
1/2 teaspoon pepper
1/2 teaspoon paprika

6 tablespoons butter
8 oz. fresh mushrooms, sliced
2 tablespoons all-purpose flour
2/3 cup chicken broth
3 tablespoons sherry
1 teaspoon dried leaf rosemary
Hot cooked wild rice

Preheat oven to 375F (190C). Cook frozen artichoke hearts according to package directions; drain and set aside. Rinse, drain and halve canned artichoke hearts; set aside. Wash chicken; pat dry with paper towels. Cut apart legs and thighs. Sprinkle chicken with salt, pepper and paprika. In a large heavy skillet, melt 1/4 cup butter. Add chicken pieces, a few at a time, and brown on both sides; remove to a 2-quart casserole. When all chicken is browned, melt remaining 2 tablespoons butter in skillet. Add mushrooms; sauté 3 minutes. Sprinkle flour over mushrooms; stir in chicken broth, sherry and rosemary. Cook, stirring constantly, until thickened. Arrange artichoke hearts between chicken pieces in casserole. Pour broth mixture over chicken and artichokes. Bake, covered, 40 minutes or until chicken is tender. Serve chicken and sauce over hot cooked wild rice. Makes 4 to 6 servings.

Sweet & Sour Chicken Legs

This recipe turns chicken legs into an Oriental-style meal.

6 chicken legs with thighs attached
1/3 cup all-purpose flour
1/4 cup vegetable oil
1 bunch green onions, thinly sliced,
   including tops
3 large garlic cloves, minced
3 tablespoons sugar
2 tablespoons grated fresh gingerroot
1 tablespoon paprika
1 tablespoon ground turmeric
1 teaspoon ground coriander

1/4 teaspoon ground cardamom
1/4 teaspoon black pepper
1/4 teaspoon red (cayenne) pepper
1/3 cup red-wine vinegar
1-1/2 cups chicken broth
1 cup uncooked long-grain white rice
2 tablespoons toasted sesame seeds
1 lemon, sliced paper thin
Chutney, chopped green onion, chopped
   cucumber, chopped tomato and peanuts

Preheat oven to 350F (175C). Wash chicken; pat dry with paper towels. Place flour on a large plate; roll chicken in flour until coated. Set aside. In a medium skillet, heat oil. Add green onions and garlic; sauté 2 minutes or until onions are limp. Stir in sugar, gingerroot, paprika, turmeric, coriander, cardamom, black pepper, red pepper, vinegar and chicken broth. Cook over medium heat 10 minutes. Add rice; stir until mixture simmers. Turn into a shallow 3-quart casserole or 13" x 9" baking dish. Top with floured chicken pieces. Turn each piece of chicken around once so it is moistened on all sides. Bake, covered, 45 minutes or until chicken is tender. Top with toasted sesame seeds and garnish with lemon slices. Serve with chutney, green onion, cucumber, tomato and peanuts as condiments. Makes 6 servings.

Chicken à l'Orange

Fruity orange sauce complements the mild flavor of chicken.

1 (3-lb.) chicken, cut up, or
   3 lbs. chicken legs and thighs
1-1/2 teaspoons salt
1/4 teaspoon black pepper
1/4 teaspoon paprika
1/4 cup all-purpose flour
2 tablespoons butter, melted
1 bunch green onions, thinly sliced,
   including tops

4 green bell peppers,
   thinly sliced into rings
1 cup fresh mushrooms, sliced
1 (6-oz.) can thawed, frozen,
   orange-juice concentrate
1/4 cup sherry
2 teaspoons grated orange peel
1 tablespoon cornstarch

Preheat oven to 350F (175C). Wash chicken; pat dry with paper towels. Cut apart legs and thighs. On a large plate, mix salt, black pepper, paprika and flour. Roll chicken in flour mixture until coated. Arrange in a single layer in a shallow 3-quart casserole or 13" x 9" baking dish. Brush with melted butter. Top with green onions, peppers and mushrooms. In a small bowl, blend orange juice, sherry, orange peel and cornstarch. Pour evenly over chicken mixture. Bake, uncovered, 1 hour or until tender; baste 3 or 4 times during cooking. Makes 6 servings.

Herbed Chicken with Asparagus

Start this meal with a fresh-tomato soup.

4 chicken-breast halves, skinned, boned
1/4 cup butter
Salt and pepper to taste
1 teaspoon fines herbes or
    Herbes de Provence
1/2 cup chicken broth
1/2 cup sliced fresh mushrooms

1 tablespoon all-purpose flour
1/2 cup whipping cream
1 teaspoon lemon juice
8 oz. fresh asparagus spears, cooked,
    drained, or 1 (10-oz.) pkg. frozen
    asparagus spears, cooked, drained
3 tablespoons shredded sharp Cheddar cheese

Preheat oven to 400F (205C). Butter a shallow 1-1/2- to 2-quart casserole. Wash chicken breasts; pat dry with paper towels. Place chicken-breast pieces between sheets of plastic wrap. Pound with the flat side of a meat mallet until thin and about 6 inches across. In a large skillet, melt 2 tablespoons butter. Add chicken; cook quickly over high heat about 1 minute on each side or until lightly browned. Sprinkle chicken with salt, pepper and herbs; remove from skillet. Pour broth into skillet; bring to a boil, stirring constantly to scrape up meat drippings. Strain broth mixture; set aside. In same skillet, melt remaining butter. Add mushrooms; sauté 5 minutes or until browned. Add flour; stir until mushrooms are lightly coated. Stir in broth mixture and cream; bring to a boil, stirring constantly until thickened. Add lemon juice. Add asparagus and heat through. To assemble casserole, place cooked chicken in bottom of buttered casserole. Spoon vegetables and sauce over chicken; sprinkle with cheese. Bake, uncovered, 10 minutes or until bubbly and cheese is melted. Makes 4 servings.

Coq au Vin

This is a standard dish in French country cooking.

1 (3- to 4-lb.) chicken, cut up, or
    3 to 4 lbs. chicken legs and thighs
2 tablespoons all-purpose flour
3 tablespoons vegetable shortening
1 small onion, chopped
3 cups Burgundy
3 cups chicken broth
1 bay leaf
1 parsley sprig

1 teaspoon dried leaf marjoram
1 teaspoon dried leaf thyme
1 garlic clove, minced
1 lb. small white onions, peeled
8 oz. fresh, small, whole mushrooms,
    stems trimmed
1/2 teaspoon salt
Buttered, toasted, French-bread slices

Preheat oven to 350F (175C). Wash chicken; pat dry with paper towels. Cut apart legs and thighs. Rub chicken with flour; set aside. In a heavy 3- to 4-quart Dutch oven, melt shortening. Add chopped onion; sauté 3 minutes or until translucent. Add chicken pieces, a few at a time, and brown on both sides. Pour in Burgundy and broth. Add bay leaf, parsley, marjoram, thyme, garlic, whole onions, mushrooms and salt. Bake, covered, 45 minutes or until chicken is tender. Remove and discard bay leaf and parsley sprig. Garnish with buttered, toasted, French-bread slices. Makes 6 servings.

Rosemary Chicken & Rice

For the cook in a hurry, this can be assembled quickly.

1 (2-1/2- to 3-lb.) chicken, cut up, or
   2-1/2 to 3 lbs. chicken legs and
   thighs
1 cup uncooked long-grain brown rice
3 garlic cloves, minced
2-1/2 cups chicken broth or water

1 teaspoon salt
1 teaspoon dried leaf rosemary
2 tablespoons lemon juice
1/4 cup mayonnaise
1/4 cup fine dry breadcrumbs
1/2 cup grated Parmesan cheese (1-1/2 oz.)

Preheat oven to 350F (175C). Butter a shallow 3-quart casserole or 13'' x 9'' baking dish. Wash chicken; pat dry with paper towels. Cut apart legs and thighs. Spread rice evenly in buttered casserole; sprinkle garlic over rice. Pour broth or water over rice mixture. Arrange chicken pieces on top. Sprinkle with salt, rosemary and lemon juice. Brush or spread mayonnaise over chicken pieces; sprinkle with breadcrumbs. Bake, uncovered, 1 to 1-1/4 hours or until chicken and rice are tender. To serve, sprinkle with Parmesan cheese. Makes 4 servings.

Chicken Cacciatore

This is even better warmed up on the second day!

2 tablespoons butter
1/2 cup olive oil
1 small onion, sliced
12 oz. fresh mushrooms, sliced
1 (3-lb.) chicken, cut up, or
   3 lbs. chicken legs and thighs
2 garlic cloves, minced
1 (16-oz.) can whole tomatoes

1-1/2 teaspoons salt
1 teaspoon dried leaf oregano
1/2 teaspoon pepper
1 teaspoon chopped fresh parsley
Additional chopped fresh parsley
Parmesan cheese
Hot cooked pasta

Preheat oven to 350F (175C). In a heavy 2-1/2- to 3-quart Dutch oven, heat butter and 1/4 cup oil. Add onion and mushrooms; sauté about 10 minutes or until tender. Remove and set aside. Wash chicken; pat dry with paper towels. Cut apart legs and thighs. Add remaining oil and garlic to Dutch oven. Add chicken pieces, a few at a time, and brown on both sides; remove to a large plate. Return chicken, onion and mushrooms to Dutch oven. Add tomatoes with juice, salt, oregano, pepper and 1 teaspoon chopped parsley. Bake, covered, 45 minutes to 1 hour or until chicken is tender. Garnish with additional chopped parsley. Serve with Parmesan cheese over hot cooked pasta. Makes 6 servings.

Sliced and cut-up turkey parts are increasingly available and make great substitutes for chicken in recipes.

How to Make Rosemary Chicken & Rice

1/Arrange chicken on rice and broth in casserole. Sprinkle with salt, rosemary and lemon juice. Brush mayonnaise over chicken pieces.

2/Sprinkle breadcrumbs over mayonnaise-coated chicken pieces.

Country Captain

This dish was brought to our eastern shores by spice traders.

1 (3-lb.) chicken, cut up, or 3 lbs. chicken legs and thighs 1/4 cup butter 1 cup blanched whole almonds 1 green bell pepper, chopped 1 garlic clove, chopped 1 medium onion, chopped	1-1/2 teaspoons curry powder 1 (16-oz.) can whole tomatoes 1 tablespoon chopped fresh parsley 1/4 teaspoon dried leaf thyme 3 tablespoons currants or raisins 4 bacon slices, crisp-cooked, crumbled

Preheat oven to 350F (175C). Wash chicken; pat dry with paper towels. Cut apart legs and thighs. In a large heavy skillet, melt butter. Add chicken pieces, a few at a time, and brown on both sides; remove to a 2-1/2-quart casserole. When all chicken is browned, add almonds to skillet; sauté in drippings until browned. Set aside. Add pepper, garlic and onion to same skillet; sauté until tender. In a medium bowl, combine curry powder, tomatoes with juice, parsley and thyme. Add to skillet; bring to a boil, stirring constantly to scrape up chicken drippings. Pour over chicken in casserole. Bake, covered, 45 minutes to 1 hour or until chicken is very tender. Pour off juices from casserole into skillet. Sprinkle almonds and currants or raisins over chicken. Bring chicken juices to a boil; boil until reduced by about half. Pour over chicken mixture in casserole. Garnish with bacon. Makes 4 to 6 servings.

Chicken Biriyani

This classic South African dish demonstrates the Indian influence in that area.

2 tablespoons vegetable oil
2 medium onions, thinly sliced
1 (3-1/2-lb.) chicken, cut up, or
   3-1/2 lbs. chicken legs and thighs
Yogurt Marinade, see below
2 tomatoes, peeled, seeded, diced
2 (3-inch) cinnamon sticks

4 cardamom pods
1 cup lentils
1 teaspoon salt
4 cups water
1 cup uncooked long-grain white rice
3 hard-cooked eggs, quartered
Chopped fresh parsley

Yogurt Marinade:
Pinch of saffron threads
2 teaspoons hot water
2 garlic cloves
1 (2-inch) piece fresh gingerroot
1/2 pint plain yogurt (1 cup)

1 teaspoon ground cumin
1/2 teaspoon ground turmeric
1 (4-oz.) can green chilies
1 tablespoon chopped fresh mint leaves

In a large skillet, heat oil. Add onions; sauté until golden. Set aside. Wash chicken; pat dry with paper towels. Cut apart legs and thighs. Place chicken in a large bowl. Prepare Yogurt Marinade. Pour marinade over chicken; mix to coat chicken completely. Top with tomatoes, 1 cinnamon stick and seeds from 2 cardamom pods. Marinate 1 hour at room temperature. Preheat oven to 350F (175C). In a medium saucepan, place lentils, salt, water, rice, 1 cinnamon stick and seeds from 2 cardamom pods. Bring to a boil; simmer 10 minutes. Remove and discard cinnamon stick. Pour cooked lentil mixture and any remaining liquid in bottom of a 4-quart casserole. Arrange chicken and sautéed onions over lentil mixture; spoon marinade over top. Bake, covered, 1 hour or until chicken is tender. Remove and discard cinnamon stick. Garnish with quartered hard-cooked eggs and parsley. Makes 6 servings.

Yogurt Marinade:
In a small bowl, soak saffron in water 5 minutes. Place saffron with water and remaining ingredients in a blender; process until smooth.

Sesame-Paprika Baked Chicken

Bake along with Curried Rice & Carrots, page 138, and serve together.

1 (3- to 3-1/2-lb.) chicken, cut up, or
   3 to 3-1/2 lbs. chicken legs and thighs
1 teaspoon paprika

1 teaspoon salt
1 teaspoon sugar
1 tablespoon sesame seeds

Preheat oven to 400F (205C). Butter a shallow 3-quart casserole or 13" x 9" baking dish. Wash chicken; pat dry with paper towels. Cut apart legs and thighs. Arrange chicken pieces, skin-side up, in buttered casserole. In a small bowl, mix paprika, salt and sugar. Sprinkle evenly over chicken. Sprinkle with sesame seeds. Bake, uncovered, 45 minutes or until chicken is browned and tender. Makes 6 servings.

How to Make Chicken Biriyani

1/Pour marinade over chicken. Top with tomatoes, 1 cinnamon stick and seeds from 2 cardamom pods. Marinate 1 hour at room temperature.

2/Arrange chicken and sautéed onions on lentil mixture in a 4-quart casserole. Spoon marinade over chicken. Bake until chicken is tender.

Chicken Provençal   Photo on cover.

Typical flavors of the south of France distinguish this dish.

**1 (3-lb.) chicken, cut up, or
  3 lbs. chicken legs and thighs
1/2 cup all-purpose flour
2-1/2 teaspoons salt
1/2 teaspoon black pepper
1/2 cup olive oil
1/2 cup chopped green bell pepper
12 small white onions, peeled
1/4 cup chopped green onion**

**4 garlic cloves, minced
3 tablespoons chopped fresh parsley
1/2 cup dry white wine
1 cup chicken broth
1 bay leaf
6 medium tomatoes, peeled, seeded,
  cut in strips
1/2 cup halved black olives
1/4 teaspoon dried leaf thyme**

Preheat oven to 350F (175C). Wash chicken pieces; pat dry with paper towels. Cut apart legs and thighs. On a large plate, mix flour, 1/2 teaspoon salt and 1/4 teaspoon black pepper. Roll chicken in flour mixture until coated. In a large skillet, heat oil. Add chicken pieces, a few at a time, and brown on both sides; remove to a shallow 2-quart casserole. When all chicken is browned, remove all but 1 tablespoon oil from skillet. Add green pepper, white onions, green onion and garlic; sauté 5 minutes, stirring constantly. Add 2 tablespoons parsley, wine, broth, bay leaf, tomatoes, olives, thyme, and remaining salt and black pepper. Pour tomato mixture over chicken in casserole. Bake, uncovered, 45 minutes or until tender. Garnish with remaining parsley. Makes 4 servings.

Crab-Stuffed Turkey Breasts

To save money, skin and bone the turkey breast yourself.

2-1/2 to 3 lbs. boneless turkey breast or
   2 lbs. turkey-breast fillets
1/4 cup butter
1/2 cup thinly sliced green onion,
   including tops
4 oz. mushrooms, thinly sliced
3 tablespoons all-purpose flour
2 teaspoons dried leaf thyme
1/2 cup chicken broth

1/2 cup half and half or whole milk
1/2 cup dry white wine
Salt and pepper to taste
2 (6-oz.) pkgs. thawed, frozen,
   snow crabmeat, drained
1/2 cup finely chopped fresh parsley
1 cup shredded Swiss cheese (4 oz.)
Hot cooked wild rice, if desired
Buttered steamed asparagus, if desired

Lightly butter a shallow 3-quart casserole. Wash turkey; pat dry with paper towels. Remove and discard skin from turkey breast; cut meat crosswise into 1/2-inch slices. Place slices or fillets between sheets of plastic wrap or waxed paper. Pound with the flat side of a meat mallet until thin and about tripled in size; set aside. In a large skillet, melt butter. Add green onion and mushrooms; sauté about 5 minutes or until soft. Stir in flour and 1 teaspoon thyme until blended. Whisk in broth, half and half or milk, and wine; bring to a boil, whisking constantly until thickened. Add salt and pepper; set aside. Preheat oven to 350F (175C). In a small bowl, combine 1/4 cup sauce, crabmeat, parsley and remaining 1 teaspoon thyme. Divide mixture among turkey-breast pieces. Roll up tightly into bundles. Place bundles, seam-side down, in buttered casserole. Spoon remaining sauce over turkey bundles; sprinkle with cheese. Bake, covered, 30 minutes or until turkey is tender. Serve with hot cooked wild rice and buttered steamed asparagus, if desired. Makes 6 servings.

Mexican Turkey Mole

Chocolate is the surprise ingredient in this classic dish.

2 pieces boneless turkey breast (5 lbs.)
2 tablespoons lard
2 large onions, chopped
3 garlic cloves, minced
4 cups chicken broth or water
1 oz. unsweetened chocolate
2 to 3 tablespoons chili powder
3 tablespoons all-purpose flour

1 teaspoon ground cinnamon
1/4 teaspoon ground cloves
1/4 teaspoon star-anise seeds
2 teaspoons salt
1/2 teaspoon pepper
1/4 cup chopped peanuts
1/4 cup toasted sesame seeds
Chopped fresh cilantro (coriander)

Preheat oven to 350F (175C). Wash turkey; pat dry with paper towels. Set aside. In a 3- to 4-quart Dutch oven, melt lard. Add onions and garlic; sauté 3 minutes. Remove with a slotted spoon; set aside. Add more lard, if needed. Add turkey breast; brown on both sides. Arrange sautéed onions and garlic on top of turkey. Heat 1 cup broth or water; place in a small bowl. Add chocolate; stir until melted. Stir in chili powder, flour, cinnamon, cloves, anise seeds, salt and pepper until blended. Pour remaining 3 cups broth or water over turkey in casserole, then add broth with seasonings. Bake, covered, 1 to 1-1/4 hours or until turkey is tender or a meat thermometer inserted in meat registers 180F (80C). Garnish with peanuts, sesame seeds and cilantro. Makes 6 servings.

Crab-Stuffed Turkey Breasts

Turkey Divine

You may want to cook a turkey just to have it for this delicious dish!

2 lbs. fresh broccoli
Creamy Cheese Sauce, see below
4 oz. thinly sliced cooked ham

1 lb. sliced cooked turkey breast
1/4 cup grated Parmesan cheese (3/4 oz.)

Creamy Cheese Sauce:
1/4 cup butter
1/4 cup all-purpose flour
1 cup chicken broth
1/2 pint half and half (1 cup)
1 teaspoon salt

1/8 teaspoon ground nutmeg
1/2 cup grated Parmesan cheese (1-1/2 oz.)
1/2 cup shredded Swiss cheese (2 oz.)
Dash of red (cayenne) pepper

Cut off and discard tough ends from broccoli stalks. Peel remaining stalks if skin is tough. Cut stalks into even pieces. In a large saucepan, cook broccoli in boiling salted water about 12 minutes or until crisp-tender; drain and set aside. Prepare Creamy Cheese Sauce. Preheat oven to 350F (175C). Butter a shallow 3-quart casserole. Arrange broccoli in buttered casserole. Cover with sliced ham, then sliced turkey. Pour Creamy Cheese Sauce over turkey; sprinkle with Parmesan cheese. Bake, uncovered, 15 minutes or until sauce is bubbly. Makes 6 servings.

Creamy Cheese Sauce:
In a medium saucepan, melt butter. Stir in flour until smooth. Cook over low heat 3 minutes, stirring constantly. Whisk in chicken broth and half and half; bring to a boil, whisking constantly until thickened and smooth. Stir in remaining ingredients. Makes 3 cups.

Scalloped Turkey with Cheddar Cheese

This is a great party dish; serve it with Waldorf salad.

4 cups water
4 chicken bouillon cubes
2 cups uncooked long-grain white rice
1/2 cup butter
2 cups sliced fresh mushrooms
2 tablespoons chopped green onion
6 tablespoons all-purpose flour
Salt to taste

1/4 teaspoon pepper
1/2 teaspoon dried leaf marjoram
1 qt. milk (4 cups)
4 cups shredded Cheddar cheese (1 lb.)
1 (2-oz.) jar chopped pimentos, drained
4 cups chopped cooked turkey
6 bread slices, crusts removed
1/4 cup butter

Butter 2 (2-quart) casseroles. In a medium saucepan, bring water to a boil with bouillon cubes; stir until bouillon cubes are dissolved. Stir in rice. Bring back to a boil. Cover and reduce heat to low. Cook 20 minutes or until rice is tender and has absorbed all the liquid; set aside. Preheat oven to 375F (190C). In a medium saucepan, melt 1/2 cup butter. Add mushrooms and green onion; sauté 5 minutes. Stir in flour, salt, pepper and marjoram until blended. Remove from heat; gradually stir in milk. Bring to a boil, stirring constantly 1 minute or until thickened. Stir in 3 cups cheese and pimentos; stir until cheese melts. Stir in turkey and cooked rice. Turn into buttered casseroles. Sprinkle with remaining cheese. Cut bread into small cubes. In a large skillet, melt 1/4 cup butter. Add bread cubes; toss in butter until golden. Arrange around edges of casseroles. Bake, uncovered, 20 minutes or until heated through and bubbly. Makes 12 servings.

Turkey Tetrazzini

This dish was created to honor Luisa Tetrazzini, an opera star.

6 tablespoons butter
5 tablespoons all-purpose flour
2-1/2 cups chicken broth
1-1/2 cups half and half
1/2 cup white wine
1-1/2 cups grated Parmesan cheese
   (4-1/2 oz.)

12 oz. fresh mushrooms, sliced
1 (12-oz.) pkg. vermicelli
3 to 4 cups slivered cooked turkey
Salt to taste

In a medium saucepan, melt 2 tablespoons butter. Stir in flour until smooth. Whisk in broth, half and half and wine. Bring to a boil, whisking constantly until thickened and smooth. Stir in 1/2 cup Parmesan cheese. Measure 1 cup sauce into a small bowl; stir in 1/2 cup Parmesan cheese. In a large skillet, melt remaining 1/4 cup butter. Add mushrooms; sauté until lightly browned. Set aside, reserving 1/2 cup in a small bowl. Cook vermicelli according to package directions until tender but firm to the bite; drain. Preheat oven to 375F (190C). Lightly butter a 2-1/2- to 3-quart casserole. In a large bowl, combine large portion of sauce, large portion of mushrooms, hot vermicelli and turkey; add salt. Turn into buttered casserole; spoon reserved 1 cup sauce evenly over surface. Sprinkle with remaining Parmesan cheese and top with reserved cooked mushroom slices. Bake, uncovered, 15 to 20 minutes or until heated through and bubbly. Preheat broiler; broil 5 inches from heat until lightly browned. Makes 6 to 8 servings.

Turkey & Wild-Rice Casserole

A great way to get the most from leftover turkey or chicken!

1 cup uncooked wild rice or half wild rice
   and half brown rice
2-1/2 cups water
1 teaspoon salt
1/4 cup butter
8 oz. fresh mushrooms, sliced
1/2 cup chopped green onion
1/2 cup sliced celery
1/4 cup all-purpose flour

1 cup chicken broth
1-1/2 cups half and half
3 cups cubed cooked turkey or chicken
1 tablespoon chopped pimento
1 tablespoon minced fresh parsley
1 teaspoon salt
1/8 teaspoon white pepper
1/8 teaspoon ground nutmeg
1/2 cup toasted slivered almonds

Preheat oven to 350F (175C). Butter a 2-quart casserole. Rinse rice in 3 changes of hot tap water or until water is no longer cloudy. In a medium saucepan, bring water and 1 teaspoon salt to a boil; stir in rice. Bring back to a boil. Cover and reduce heat to low. Cook 35 to 40 minutes or until rice is tender and has absorbed all the liquid; set aside. In a large skillet, melt butter. Add mushrooms, green onion and celery; sauté 5 minutes or until celery is crisp-tender. Stir in flour until blended. Whisk in chicken broth and half and half; cook, stirring constantly until thickened. Add chicken or turkey. Add rice to chicken or turkey mixture with pimento, parsley, 1 teaspoon salt, white pepper and nutmeg. Turn into buttered casserole. Bake, covered, 45 minutes or until heated through and bubbly. Garnish with almonds. Makes 4 to 6 servings.

Fish & Seafood

It's so easy to prepare a delicious quick casserole using frozen blocks of fish! There are several recipes in this chapter that depend on this most commonly available form of fish. Scottish Cod with Mustard Sauce, Cod Alla Marinara, Fillet of Sole in White Wine & Herbs, Country Cod and Quick Fish Bake are all examples of tasty and economical main dishes. You will find there is a difference in cooking times for fresh fish, frozen fish blocks and individually frozen fillets. The range is given in the recipe.

Canned fish and seafood can become an elegant entree when prepared in a casserole. Salmon & Green-Olive Casserole, prepared with canned salmon, makes a suitable main dish for a smart luncheon or an excellent first course to a dinner.

Casseroles also stretch the servings of rather expensive seafood to make main dishes that are fancy enough for special entertaining. Crab Soufflé Provençal, for instance, elegantly stretches a six-ounce package of frozen crabmeat to give six delicious servings.

Two of the most flamboyant of the seafood casseroles are ideal choices for very special occasions. New Orleans Shrimp-Boat Casserole and Ann's Chilled Seafood Casserole include many costly ingredients, but make the best use of them by serving so many people.

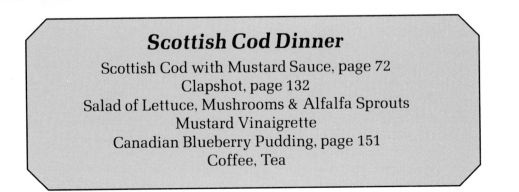

Scottish Cod Dinner

Scottish Cod with Mustard Sauce, page 72
Clapshot, page 132
Salad of Lettuce, Mushrooms & Alfalfa Sprouts
Mustard Vinaigrette
Canadian Blueberry Pudding, page 151
Coffee, Tea

Fillet of Sole in White Wine & Herbs

If you use frozen fish, expect the longer baking time.

2 lbs. fresh or frozen sole fillets
3 tablespoons butter, melted
1/2 cup dry white wine
1/2 cup chopped green onion
2 bay leaves, crumbled
1 teaspoon chopped fresh parsley

1 teaspoon dried leaf tarragon
1/2 teaspoon salt
1/4 teaspoon pepper
1/2 cup whipping cream
Additional chopped fresh parsley
Lemon wedges

Preheat oven to 400F (205C). Butter a shallow 2- to 2-1/2-quart casserole. Wash fresh fish; pat dry with paper towels. If using frozen fish, rinse under cold running water to wash off excess frost; pat dry with paper towels. Arrange fish in buttered casserole. If using frozen fish blocks, place them slightly apart. If using fresh fish, fillets may overlap slightly. Drizzle with butter; pour wine around fish. Sprinkle with green onion, bay leaves, 1 teaspoon chopped parsley, tarragon, salt and pepper. Bake, uncovered, 15 to 20 minutes for fresh fish or 30 to 35 minutes for frozen fish, or until fish flakes when probed gently with a fork. Strain off fish juices into a medium skillet. Bring to a boil; cook, stirring constantly until reduced by half. Whisk in cream. Bring to a boil; cook, stirring constantly until thickened and smooth. Pour sauce over fish. Garnish with additional chopped parsley. Serve with lemon wedges. Makes 4 servings.

Quick Fish Bake

A family favorite; this is quick, easy, and economical!

2 lbs. fresh or frozen fish fillets,
  such as sole, cod or haddock
1 medium onion, thinly sliced
3 medium carrots, shredded
2 tablespoons butter
2 tablespoons all-purpose flour
1 cup milk

1/4 cup white wine
1/2 to 1 teaspoon salt
1 teaspoon dried leaf thyme
1/4 cup grated Parmesan cheese (3/4 oz.)
1/8 teaspoon ground nutmeg
Chopped fresh parsley

Preheat oven to 450F (230C). Butter a shallow 2-1/2-quart casserole or 13" x 9" baking dish. Wash fresh fish; pat dry with paper towels. If using frozen fish, rinse under cold running water to wash off excess frost; pat dry with paper towels. Arrange fish in buttered casserole. If using frozen fish blocks, place them slightly apart. If using fresh fish, fillets may overlap slightly. Top with onion and carrots. In a medium saucepan, melt butter. Stir in flour until smooth. Whisk in milk; bring to a boil, whisking constantly until thickened and smooth. Stir in wine; boil 2 minutes. Stir in salt, thyme, Parmesan cheese and nutmeg. Pour sauce over fish and vegetables in casserole. Bake 15 to 20 minutes for fresh fish or 40 to 50 minutes for frozen fish, or until fish flakes when probed gently with a fork. Garnish with parsley. Makes 4 servings.

Scottish Cod with Mustard Sauce

Clapshot, page 132, is the authentic Scottish accompaniment to this dish.

4 to 6 fresh or frozen cod fillets (2 lbs.)
4 to 6 parsley sprigs
3/4 cup boiling water
1/4 cup dry white wine or
   2 tablespoons lemon juice
2 to 4 bay leaves, crumbled
6 whole peppercorns

1 teaspoon salt
Half and half or whole milk
3 tablespoons butter
1/4 cup all-purpose flour
2 teaspoons Dijon-style mustard
Chopped fresh parsley

Preheat oven to 400F (205C). Wash fresh fish; pat dry with paper towels. If using frozen fish, rinse under cold running water to wash off excess frost; pat dry with paper towels. Butter a shallow 2-1/2- to 3-quart casserole or 10-inch-square baking dish. Place parsley sprigs in buttered casserole; arrange fish in a single layer on top. Parsley will keep fish from sticking to casserole. Pour boiling water and wine or lemon juice over fish. Sprinkle crumbled bay leaves, peppercorns and salt over fish. Bake, uncovered, 15 to 20 minutes for fresh fish or 40 to 50 minutes for frozen fish, or until fish flakes when probed gently with a fork. Pour off fish juices and strain. Measure juices and add half and half or milk to make 2 cups; set aside. In a medium saucepan, melt butter. Stir in flour until smooth. Remove from heat. Whisk in fish-stock mixture until smooth. Return to heat; bring to a boil, whisking constantly until thickened. Stir in mustard. Taste and adjust seasoning, if necessary. Preheat broiler. Spoon sauce over fish in casserole. Broil about 6 inches from heat until browned in spots. Garnish with chopped parsley. Makes 4 to 6 servings.

Cod alla Marinara

Serve the delicious juices from the pan over rice or pasta.

4 fresh or frozen cod fillets (2 lbs.)
1 (16-oz.) can tomatoes,
   pressed through a sieve
1/4 cup chopped, stuffed, green olives

2 tablespoons capers
1 tablespoon chopped fresh parsley
1/2 teaspoon pepper
1/2 teaspoon dried leaf oregano

Preheat oven to 400F (205C). Wash fresh fish; pat dry with paper towels. If using frozen fish, rinse under cold running water to wash off excess frost; pat dry with paper towels. Butter a shallow 2- to 2-1/2-quart casserole or 8-inch-square baking dish. Arrange fish in a single layer in buttered casserole. In a medium saucepan, combine tomatoes, olives, capers, parsley, pepper and oregano. Bring to a boil; pour over fish. Bake, uncovered, 15 to 20 minutes for fresh fish or 40 to 50 minutes for frozen fish, or until fish flakes when probed gently with a fork. Pour off fish juices into a medium skillet. Bring to a boil; cook, stirring constantly until reduced by half. Pour over fish. Makes 4 servings.

How to Make Scottish Cod with Mustard Sauce

1/Place parsley sprigs in casserole; arrange fish in a single layer on top.

2/Bake fish until it flakes when probed gently with a fork.

Country Cod

The combined flavors of butter, onion, garlic and tomatoes taste delicious over baked cod and potatoes.

4 large potatoes, peeled
1 lb. fresh or frozen cod fillets
1/4 cup butter
1 large onion, coarsely chopped
1 large garlic clove, minced
2 large tomatoes

1 medium, green bell pepper,
  coarsely chopped
1 teaspoon salt
Black pepper to taste
1 teaspoon dried leaf thyme, crushed

Cook potatoes in boiling, salted water 10 minutes. Wash fresh fish; pat dry with paper towels. If using frozen fish, rinse under cold running water to wash off excess frost; pat dry with paper towels. Preheat oven to 400F (205C). Butter a shallow 2- to 2-1/2-quart casserole. In a large skillet, melt butter. Add onion and garlic; sauté until tender but not browned. Remove and discard core from tomatoes; chop tomatoes. Stir into onion mixture; cook 2 minutes. Stir in green pepper, salt, black pepper and thyme. Arrange fish in buttered casserole. Place partially cooked whole potatoes around fish. Pour tomato mixture over fish and potatoes. Bake, uncovered, 15 to 20 minutes for fresh fish or 40 to 50 minutes for frozen fish, or until fish flakes when probed gently with a fork. Makes 4 servings.

Salmon & Green-Olive Casserole

Great for a buffet—serve with spinach salad and hot rolls.

2 cups water
1/2 teaspoon salt
1 cup uncooked long-grain white rice
1 (16-oz.) can salmon
Half and half
1/4 cup butter
2 tablespoons chopped green onion

1/4 cup all-purpose flour
Pepper to taste
1/2 cup stuffed green olives, chopped
2 teaspoons dried dill weed
3 tablespoons fresh breadcrumbs
2 teaspoons melted butter

In a medium saucepan, bring water and salt to a boil; stir in rice. Bring back to a boil. Cover and reduce heat to low. Cook 20 minutes or until rice is tender and has absorbed all the liquid. Preheat oven to 400F (205C). Butter a shallow 2-quart casserole or 8-inch-square baking dish. Spread cooked rice over bottom of buttered casserole. Drain salmon and set aside, reserving liquid. Add enough half and half to salmon liquid to measure 2 cups; set aside. In a large skillet, melt 1/4 cup butter. Add green onion; sauté 3 minutes or until limp but not browned. Sprinkle with flour and a generous grinding of pepper. Stir half and half mixture into onion mixture in skillet. Cook over medium heat, stirring constantly until thickened. Stir in olives and dill weed. Remove and discard skin and bones from salmon. Break salmon into large pieces; arrange over rice in casserole. Pour sauce evenly over salmon mixture. In a small bowl, combine breadcrumbs and melted butter; sprinkle over salmon mixture. Bake, uncovered, 15 minutes or until heated through and bubbly. Makes 6 servings.

White Clam Sauce Baked with Linguine

This is excellent served either as a first course or main dish.

1 (1-lb.) pkg. linguine
3/4 cup olive oil
6 garlic cloves, minced
1 lb. raw clams, shucked,
   coarsely chopped

About 2 cups bottled clam juice
1/2 cup chopped fresh parsley
1-1/2 teaspoons dried leaf oregano
Salt and pepper to taste
Grated Parmesan cheese

Cook linguine according to package directions until tender but firm to the bite; drain. Rinse with cold water to prevent sticking; drain well. Butter a shallow 2-quart casserole or 8-inch-square baking dish. Spread linguine over bottom of buttered casserole; set aside. Preheat oven to 350F (175C). In a large saucepan, heat oil. Add garlic; sauté about 5 minutes or until golden. Drain clams and measure juice Add enough bottled juice to make 3 cups. Add to garlic with parsley, oregano, salt and pepper; simmer 10 minutes. Remove from heat; add clams. Pour over linguine in casserole. Sprinkle with Parmesan cheese. Bake, uncovered, 15 minutes or until heated through. Makes 8 first-course servings or 4 main-course servings.

Tuna Casserole Supreme

You may use an equal amount of any shape noodles or macaroni.

1 (10-oz.) pkg. large macaroni shells
1/4 cup butter
8 oz. fresh mushrooms, sliced
2 (6-1/2- to 7-oz.) cans tuna,
  drained, flaked
1 (10-oz.) pkg. frozen green peas
1/4 cup all-purpose flour
1 teaspoon salt

1/2 teaspoon dried dill weed
1/4 teaspoon white pepper
1 pint half and half or whole milk (2 cups)
1 cup chicken broth
3 tablespoons dry sherry, if desired
1/2 cup fresh breadcrumbs
2 tablespoons melted butter

Cook macaroni according to package directions until tender but firm to the bite; drain. Rinse with cold water to prevent sticking; drain well. Preheat oven to 350F (175C). Butter a shallow 2- to 2-1/2-quart casserole. In a large skillet, melt 1/4 cup butter. Add mushrooms; sauté over high heat 3 to 5 minutes or until tender. Arrange 1/2 of macaroni over bottom of buttered casserole. Top with 1/2 of tuna and 1/2 of peas. Using a slotted spoon, remove mushrooms from skillet, leaving drippings in skillet. Spoon mushrooms over peas. Top with remaining macaroni, tuna and peas. Whisk flour into drippings in skillet until blended. Stir in salt, dill weed, white pepper, half and half or milk, and broth; bring to a boil, whisking constantly until thickened. Whisk in sherry, if desired. Pour sauce over mixture in casserole. In a small bowl, combine breadcrumbs and melted butter; sprinkle over sauce in casserole. Bake, uncovered, 30 to 40 minutes or until browned and bubbly. Makes 6 servings.

Crispy Fish-Stick Casserole

Easy on the budget and a favorite with kids!

2 cups cooked rice
3 tablespoons butter
1 small onion, chopped
2 tablespoons minced green bell pepper
1 (8-oz.) can tomato sauce

1/2 teaspoon sugar
2 teaspoons vinegar
2 teaspoons Worcestershire sauce
1 (8-oz.) pkg. frozen fish sticks

Preheat oven to 400F (205C). Butter a shallow 1- to 1-1/2-quart casserole. Spread rice over bottom of buttered casserole; set aside. In a small saucepan, melt butter. Add onion and green pepper; sauté about 3 minutes or until onion is tender but not browned. Stir in tomato sauce, sugar, vinegar and Worcestershire sauce. Cook and stir 5 minutes. Pour sauce over rice in casserole. Arrange fish sticks over rice and tomato mixture. Bake, uncovered, 15 minutes or until fish sticks are crisp on top. Makes 4 servings.

New Orleans Shrimp-Boat Casserole

Definitely an elegant casserole for a special occasion!

2 (9-oz.) pkgs. frozen artichoke hearts or
  2 (8-1/2-oz. net dr. wt.) cans
  artichoke hearts
2 lbs. large shrimp, peeled, deveined
1/2 cup butter
8 oz. fresh mushrooms, sliced
1/4 cup all-purpose flour
1/2 pint whipping cream (1 cup)
1/2 cup milk

1 teaspoon salt
1/2 teaspoon pepper
1/4 cup dry sherry
1 tablespoon chopped fresh parsley
1 tablespoon Worcestershire sauce
1/4 cup grated Parmesan cheese (3/4 oz.)
1/4 teaspoon paprika
Hot cooked rice
Steamed zucchini and carrots, if desired

Preheat oven to 350F (175C). Butter a shallow 1-1/2-quart casserole. Cook frozen artichoke hearts according to package directions; drain. Rinse, drain and halve canned artichoke hearts. Place artichoke hearts in bottom of buttered casserole. Top with shrimp. In a medium skillet, melt 3 tablespoons butter. Add mushrooms; sauté 6 to 8 minutes or until tender. Sprinkle over shrimp in casserole. In a medium saucepan, melt remaining butter. Stir in flour until smooth. Cook over low heat 3 to 5 minutes or until lightly browned, stirring constantly. Whisk in cream and milk; bring to a boil, whisking constantly until thickened and smooth. Stir in salt, pepper, sherry, parsley and Worcestershire sauce. Pour over mixture in casserole. Top with Parmesan cheese and sprinkle with paprika. Bake, uncovered, 25 minutes or until heated through and bubbly. Serve with hot cooked rice and steamed zucchini and carrots, if desired. Makes 4 dinner servings or 6 to 8 luncheon servings.

Creole Shrimp

The secret to the sauce lies in cooking the tomato paste!

1/4 cup vegetable oil
1 (6-oz.) can tomato paste
1-1/2 cups chopped celery
1-1/2 cups chopped onion
1-1/2 cups chopped green bell pepper
1/2 cup chopped green onion
3 garlic cloves, minced

1 (15-oz.) can tomato sauce
3 bay leaves, crumbled
1 teaspoon dried leaf thyme
1 to 2 lbs. large shrimp, peeled, deveined
Dash of red (cayenne) pepper
Salt to taste
Hot cooked wild, white or brown rice

In a large heavy Dutch oven or skillet, heat oil. Add tomato paste; cook over medium heat 20 minutes, stirring constantly. Preheat oven to 300F (150C). Add celery, onion, green pepper, green onion and garlic to tomato paste. Stir in tomato sauce, bay leaves and thyme. Turn into a 2-quart casserole. Bake, covered, 2 hours. Stir in shrimp, red pepper and salt. Cover and bake 15 minutes longer or just until shrimp turn pink. Serve over hot cooked rice. Makes 6 servings.

Crab Soufflé Provençal

A great luncheon dish! Serve this with a fresh-fruit boat.

2 tablespoons butter
1 bunch green onions, minced,
   including tops
1 green bell pepper, minced
1/3 cup all-purpose flour
1 teaspoon salt
1/2 teaspoon white pepper
1 cup half and half

2 tablespoons tomato paste
Dash of red (cayenne) pepper
6 eggs, separated
1 (6-oz.) pkg. thawed frozen crabmeat,
   drained
1 cup shredded Swiss cheese (4 oz.)
1 teaspoon dried leaf tarragon

In a large saucepan, melt butter. Add green onions and green pepper; sauté about 3 minutes or until vegetables are bright green and crisp-tender. Stir in flour, salt and white pepper until blended. Stir in half and half; cook over medium-high heat, stirring constantly until thickened. Stir in tomato paste and red pepper; remove from heat. In a large bowl, beat egg whites until frothy, then beat until whites form short moist peaks; do not beat until dry and lumpy. Whisk egg yolks into sauce. Stir in crabmeat, cheese and tarragon. Preheat oven to 375F (190C). Fold about 1/4 of beaten egg whites into sauce to lighten it. Then fold remaining beaten egg whites into sauce mixture. Butter a 2-quart soufflé dish. Pour crab mixture into buttered soufflé dish. Bake 45 minutes or until top feels dry; center will have the consistency of sauce. For a firm soufflé, bake 10 minutes longer. Serve immediately. Makes 6 servings.

Note: Unbaked soufflé mixture may be held at room temperature up to 2 hours before baking or covered and refrigerated overnight. Soufflé held overnight may be slightly coarse in texture but flavor will be good.

Hot Seafood Salad

Serve as a first course or main course for brunch or lunch.

2 cups sliced celery
1/2 cup chopped green onion
1 medium, green bell pepper,
   finely chopped
1 (8-oz.) can sliced water chestnuts,
   drained
1 (6-oz.) pkg. thawed frozen crabmeat,
   drained
1 (6-oz.) pkg. thawed frozen shrimp,
   drained

8 oz. fresh mushrooms, sliced
1 cup mayonnaise
4 hard-cooked eggs, sliced
1 teaspoon dried leaf thyme
1/2 teaspoon salt
1/2 teaspoon paprika
1/2 cup fresh breadcrumbs
2 tablespoons butter, melted
Fresh spinach leaves, if desired

Preheat oven to 350F (175C). Butter a 2-quart casserole. In a large bowl, combine all ingredients except breadcrumbs, butter and spinach leaves. Fold together until blended. Turn into buttered casserole. In a small bowl, combine breadcrumbs and melted butter; sprinkle over mixture in casserole. Bake, uncovered, 30 minutes or until heated through. If served as a first course, arrange spinach leaves on plates and mound salad on top. Makes 8 first-course servings or 4 main-dish servings.

How to Make Crab Soufflé Provençal

1/In a large bowl, beat egg whites until frothy, then beat until whites form short moist peaks; do not beat until dry and lumpy.

2/Fold about 1/4 of beaten egg whites into crabmeat sauce to lighten it. Then fold remaining beaten egg whites into sauce mixture. Pour into buttered soufflé dish and bake.

Ann's Chilled Seafood Casserole

This casserole is chilled rather than baked before serving.

1 cup uncooked wild rice or brown rice
2-1/2 cups water
1 teaspoon salt
12 oz. cooked fresh crabmeat or
   2 (6-oz.) pkgs. thawed frozen crabmeat, drained
1 lb. shrimp, peeled, deveined, cooked
1/3 cup olive oil or peanut oil
3 medium, green apples, peeled, chopped
5 shallots or green onions, chopped

3 teaspoons curry powder
2 teaspoons celery seeds
2 teaspoons dry mustard
1/2 teaspoon salt
1/4 teaspoon pepper
3/4 cup dairy sour cream
2 cups mayonnaise
2 tablespoons lemon juice (1/2 lemon)
Parsley sprigs

Brush a shallow 2-quart casserole with oil. Rinse wild rice in 3 changes of hot tap water or until water is no longer cloudy. Brown rice need not be rinsed. In a medium saucepan, bring water and salt to a boil; stir in rice. Bring back to a boil. Cover and reduce heat to low. Cook 35 to 40 minutes or until rice is tender and has absorbed all the liquid. Spread rice over bottom of buttered casserole. Cover with crabmeat, then with shrimp. In a large skillet, heat oil. Add apples and shallots or green onions; sauté about 5 minutes or until tender. Stir in curry powder, celery seeds, mustard, salt and pepper; cool. Stir in sour cream, mayonnaise and lemon juice. Spread over top of seafood in casserole. Garnish with parsley. Cover and refrigerate 1 to 2 hours or overnight before serving. Makes 8 servings.

Low-Calorie Casseroles

How do you take the calories out of a casserole? One way to reduce them is to eliminate as much of the fat and carbohydrate as possible. Recipes in this chapter demonstrate how this can be done. Zucchini Lasagna is an excellent example: Zucchini slices replace the wide lasagna noodles so most of the carbohydrate has been removed. Flavors are spicy and typical of the original dish. You won't even miss the calories!

Low-calorie foods need not be bland and boring as you will see in this chapter. No need to skip the exciting ethnic meals, either. Calories are reduced in a spicy Moroccan tajine not only by cutting down on cooking fat, but by changing the original meat from beef to turkey. The surprising addition of pears is enhanced by the sweet flavor of cinnamon. The result is a delicious new recipe— Turkey Breast & Pears.

Some classic preparations, such as Korean Beef Strips, are naturally low in calories. The meat must be lean and tender. The ingredients are classic for Korean marinades—soy sauce, sesame seeds and a touch of sesame oil. Luckily for calorie-counters, a little sesame oil goes a long way. Be adventurous and try this marinade on a lean beef rump roast.

The classic Beef Bourguignonne is quite rich. However, in this lean adaptation of the original, we have left out the salt pork and other rich ingredients. Be sure to cut off all the fat on the beef, too!

Veal is a lean meat. Paprika Veal is a classic dish which is usually enriched with sour cream. In my version, I have substituted yogurt—the result is delicious!

Chicken is also naturally lean, but you can make it even more low calorie by removing the fatty skin before cooking. An added advantage is that with the skin gone, the flavors of wine and herbs can permeate the flesh.

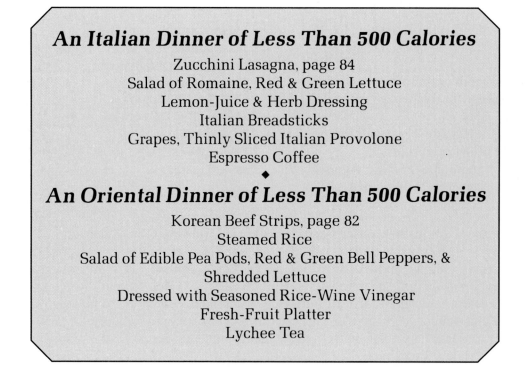

An Italian Dinner of Less Than 500 Calories

Zucchini Lasagna, page 84
Salad of Romaine, Red & Green Lettuce
Lemon-Juice & Herb Dressing
Italian Breadsticks
Grapes, Thinly Sliced Italian Provolone
Espresso Coffee

◆

An Oriental Dinner of Less Than 500 Calories

Korean Beef Strips, page 82
Steamed Rice
Salad of Edible Pea Pods, Red & Green Bell Peppers, &
Shredded Lettuce
Dressed with Seasoned Rice-Wine Vinegar
Fresh-Fruit Platter
Lychee Tea

Sole Florentine

Spinach is the classic "bed" for any Florentine dish.

2 lbs. fresh or frozen sole fillets
Herb Sauce, see below
3 (10-oz.) pkgs. frozen chopped spinach,
   cooked, drained
1 tablespoon lemon juice

1 tablespoon butter or margarine, melted
1 tablespoon dry breadcrumbs
Dash of paprika
2 green onions, sliced

Herb Sauce:
3 tablespoons butter or margarine
2 green onions, sliced
1/4 cup all-purpose flour
1 pint hot skim milk (2 cups)

1 teaspoon salt
1 teaspoon dried leaf basil
3 egg yolks

Preheat oven to 375F (190C). Wash fresh fish; pat dry with paper towels. If using frozen fish, rinse under cold running water to wash off excess frost; pat dry with paper towels. Prepare Herb Sauce. Squeeze spinach in a sieve to remove excess liquid. Blend spinach and lemon juice into Herb Sauce. Spread spinach mixture evenly over bottom of a shallow 3-quart casserole or 13" x 9" baking dish. Arrange fish on top of spinach mixture. If using frozen fish blocks, place them slightly apart. If using fresh fish, fillets may overlap slightly. Drizzle with melted butter or margarine; sprinkle with breadcrumbs and paprika. Bake, uncovered, 15 to 20 minutes for fresh fish or 30 to 35 minutes for frozen fish, or until fish flakes when probed gently with a fork. Garnish baked fish with green onions. Makes 6 servings, about 300 calories per serving.

Herb Sauce:
In small saucepan, melt butter or margarine. Add green onions; sauté 1 minute or until limp. Stir in flour until smooth. Whisk in hot milk; bring to a boil, whisking constantly until thickened and smooth. Add salt and basil. Place egg yolks in a small bowl. Stir a small amount of sauce into egg yolks. Stir egg-yolk mixture into remaining sauce in saucepan; remove from heat. Makes 2 cups.

Lean Beef Bourguignonne

Accompany this lean beef stew with a crisp green salad.

2 teaspoons olive oil
1 medium onion, thinly sliced
1 lb. lean boneless beef top round,
   cut in 1-inch squares
1/2 cup dry Burgundy

1/2 cup beef broth
1/2 teaspoon salt
1/2 teaspoon pepper
1-1/2 lbs. fresh, small, whole mushrooms
Chopped fresh parsley

In a large heavy skillet, heat 1 teaspoon oil. Add onion; sauté until limp. Remove to a 2-quart casserole. Heat remaining oil in skillet. Add meat pieces, a few at a time, and brown on all sides; remove to casserole. When all meat is browned, pour wine into skillet. Bring to a boil, stirring constantly to scrape up meat drippings. Pour over meat in casserole; add beef broth, salt and pepper. Bake, covered, in a 300F (150C) oven 1 hour or until meat is tender. Drain juices from casserole into skillet; bring to a boil. Add mushrooms; cook and stir until juices have reduced to a glaze and mushrooms look shiny. There will be about 1/2 cup glaze. Pour mushrooms and sauce over meat in casserole. Garnish with parsley. Makes 4 servings, about 225 calories per serving.

Korean Beef Strips

Toasted sesame seeds characterize the soy marinade of Korea.

2 tablespoons sesame seeds
1 lb. beef sirloin, top round or tenderloin
2 tablespoons soy sauce
2 tablespoons water
2 tablespoons sliced green onion,
   including tops

1/4 teaspoon sesame oil
2 teaspoons sugar
1 garlic clove, minced
Dash of pepper

Place meat in freezer 30 minutes to make it easier to slice. Place sesame seeds in a small heavy skillet. Stir over medium heat 5 to 10 minutes or until golden brown. Crush with a mortar and pestle or process in a blender. Cut partially frozen meat, across the grain, into 1/4-inch slices. In a shallow 2-quart casserole or 8-inch-square baking dish, arrange meat slices in a single layer. In a small bowl, combine soy sauce, water, green onion, toasted sesame seeds, sesame oil, sugar, garlic and pepper. Pour over meat. Marinate 30 minutes to 1 hour at room temperature or in refrigerator overnight, turning meat slices over once. Preheat oven to 400F (205C). Bake, uncovered, 10 to 15 minutes or until meat is tender. Tenderloin will take 10 minutes to cook to rare. Makes 4 servings, about 200 calories per serving.

Chicken Baked in Wine & Herbs

All the fat has been eliminated from the original version.

1 (3-lb.) chicken, cut up, skinned, or
   3 lbs. chicken legs and thighs, skinned
1/2 lemon
1/3 cup Cognac or brandy
2 cups light Burgundy or rosé
2 whole garlic cloves, bruised, peeled
2 bay leaves

1 tablespoon dried leaf basil
1 tablespoon chopped fresh parsley
1 tablespoon dried leaf thyme
1 teaspoon salt
Pepper to taste
8 oz. fresh, small, whole mushrooms
8 oz. small white onions, peeled, boiled

Preheat broiler. Wash chicken; pat dry with paper towels. Rub each chicken piece with cut side of lemon. Pack, fleshy-side up, close together in a shallow baking dish. Broil 3 inches from heat 2-1/2 to 3 minutes or until top of chicken is flecked with brown. Turn over and broil on other side. Remove from broiler. Preheat oven to 350F (175C). Pack chicken pieces in bottom of a 2-quart casserole. In a small saucepan, warm Cognac or brandy over low heat until bubbles begin to appear around edge of pan. Using a long match, carefully ignite brandy. Pour over chicken. Pour Burgundy or rosé over chicken; it should cover chicken by about 1/2 inch. Add garlic, bay leaves, basil, parsley, thyme, salt and pepper. Add mushrooms and onions. Bake, covered, 1 hour or until chicken is tender. Remove and discard bay leaves. Drain juices from casserole into a medium skillet; bring to a boil. Cook and stir until juices are reduced to a glaze, about 3/4 cup. Pour over chicken and vegetables. Makes 4 servings, 275 to 300 calories per serving.

How to Make Korean Beef Strips

1/Cut meat, across the grain, into 1/4-inch slices. Arrange meat slices in a single layer in a shallow 2-quart casserole.

2/Pour marinade over meat; marinate 30 minutes to 1 hour at room temperature or in refrigerator overnight. Bake until tender.

Turkey Breast & Pears

This stew-like casserole tastes like the calorie count is higher than it is!

3 lbs. boneless turkey breast, skinned,
    cut in 1-inch cubes
1 teaspoon butter or margarine
1 large onion, chopped
3 garlic cloves, minced
2 tablespoons chopped fresh cilantro
    (coriander)
2 teaspoons grated fresh gingerroot
1 teaspoon salt

Black pepper to taste
1 teaspoon ground turmeric
1/4 teaspoon red (cayenne) pepper
1 (3-inch) cinnamon stick
2 fresh Bartlett pears, peeled,
    quartered, cored
1 tablespoon honey
2 teaspoons lime juice
Ground cinnamon

Preheat oven to 325F (165C). In a heavy 3- to 4-quart Dutch oven, turn turkey-breast pieces in butter or margarine; heat through, but do not brown. Add onion, garlic, cilantro, gingerroot, salt, black pepper, turmeric, red pepper and cinnamon stick. Bake, covered, 1 hour. Add pears to Dutch oven; drizzle with honey and lime juice. Bake, uncovered, 30 minutes longer or until turkey is tender. Remove and discard cinnamon stick. Dust with ground cinnamon. Makes 6 servings, about 235 calories per serving.

Zucchini Lasagna

Zucchini replaces pasta to reduce the total calorie count.

1 lb. extra-lean ground beef
1 medium onion, finely chopped
1 garlic clove, minced
1 (15-oz.) can tomato sauce
1 teaspoon salt
1 teaspoon dried leaf basil
1 teaspoon dried leaf oregano
1/2 teaspoon dried leaf thyme

1/2 teaspoon dried leaf marjoram
1-1/2 cups dry cottage cheese
1/2 cup grated Parmesan cheese (1-1/2 oz.)
1 egg
4 medium zucchini
2 tablespoons all-purpose flour
1 cup shredded mozzarella cheese (4 oz.)

In a large skillet, brown beef with onion and garlic; drain off any fat. Stir in tomato sauce, salt, basil, oregano, thyme and marjoram; simmer, uncovered, 10 minutes. In a small bowl, combine cottage cheese, 1/2 of Parmesan cheese and egg; set aside. Scrub zucchini; slice lengthwise into 1/8-inch-thick slices. Preheat oven to 350F (175C). Lightly oil a 13" x 9" baking dish. Layer 1/2 of zucchini in oiled baking dish; sprinkle with 1/2 of flour. Top with 1/2 of cottage-cheese mixture and 1/2 of meat mixture, then with 1/2 of mozzarella cheese. Top with remaining zucchini; sprinkle with remaining flour. Top with remaining cottage-cheese mixture, meat mixture and mozzarella cheese. Sprinkle remaining Parmesan cheese over top. Bake, uncovered, 1 hour. Let stand 20 minutes before serving. Cut into 9 squares. Makes 9 servings, about 240 calories per serving.

Paprika Veal

Instead of rice, try serving this on shredded iceberg lettuce!

1 lb. veal stew cubes
1/2 teaspoon salt
Pepper to taste
1 bacon slice, cut in 1/4-inch strips
2 small onions, chopped
1 garlic clove, minced
8 oz. fresh mushrooms, quartered

1 tomato, peeled, seeded, diced
1 tablespoon mild or hot Hungarian paprika
3/4 cup chicken broth
2 tablespoons dry sherry
1/4 cup plain yogurt
Chopped fresh parsley

Preheat oven to 350F (175C). Sprinkle veal with salt and pepper. In a large heavy skillet, cook bacon until crisp; drain. Remove to a 1-1/2-quart casserole. Add seasoned veal, a few pieces at a time, to skillet with bacon drippings; brown on all sides. Remove to casserole. When all veal is browned, add onions and garlic to skillet; sauté 5 minutes or until tender. Remove to casserole. Add mushrooms to skillet; sauté until browned. Remove to casserole. Sprinkle tomato and paprika over veal mixture in casserole. Pour chicken broth and sherry into skillet; bring to a boil, stirring constantly to scrape up meat drippings. Pour over veal mixture in casserole. Bake, covered, 1 hour. Drain juices from casserole into skillet; bring to a boil. Cook and stir until juices are reduced to a glaze, about 1/2 cup. Stir yogurt into reduced juices; pour over veal mixture. Garnish with parsley. Makes 4 servings, about 225 calories per serving.

How to Make Zucchini Lasagna

1/Layer 1/2 of zucchini in baking dish; sprinkle with 1/2 of flour.

2/Continue layering cottage-cheese mixture, meat mixture, mozzarella cheese and zucchini. Sprinkle Parmesan cheese over final layer of mozzarella. Bake 1 hour.

Tofu, Spinach & Shrimp Bake

Tofu, a cheese-like curd made from soybeans, is high in protein but low in calories.

4 oz. tofu
2 eggs
1 (10-oz.) pkg. thawed, frozen,
  chopped spinach, drained
1 garlic clove, minced
1/2 teaspoon dried leaf thyme

1/2 teaspoon salt
1/2 cup chopped fresh mushrooms
1/4 cup chopped onion
3 green onions, sliced
4 oz. shrimp, peeled, deveined

Preheat oven to 350F (175C). In a medium bowl, mix tofu and eggs until well-blended; set aside. In a medium, non-stick skillet, combine spinach, garlic, thyme, salt, mushrooms, onion and green onions. Sauté 10 minutes or until vegetables are tender and liquid has evaporated. Remove from heat; add tofu mixture and shrimp. Turn into a shallow 1-quart casserole. Bake, uncovered, 25 minutes or until set. Makes 2 servings, about 215 calories per serving.

Casseroles for Two

People who cook for two tend to be on one end or the other of the age spectrum. Young couples and singles begin their independent lives cooking for one or two. As the family grows, cooking and entertaining tends to be for larger numbers, with an occasional "dinner for two," if you plan it right. When the family leaves home, most meals are for two once again.

Cooking for two can be a challenge or a delight depending on how you look at it. To avoid an entire diet of short-order cooking, you will need to plan ahead.

Although it may seem that casserole cookery isn't for the small-volume cook, look again! In addition to the recipes in this chapter which are designed for just two, full-size casseroles can also work for you.

Casseroles by their nature are normally made of homogeneous ingredients. Once baked and served, the remainder is easily packaged and frozen in smaller serving portions. During the testing of this book, I have packaged casseroles in portions to serve two. Heavy-duty plastic bags are ideal because they can be stacked. Properly labelled and categorized, you can pick out what you want from the freezer when you want a quick and easy meal. It's a good idea to add the oven temperature and baking time to the label to save looking up the original recipe. Stored at zero degrees, casseroles keep several weeks.

To reheat frozen casseroles, place the thawed food in an ovenproof baking dish. Cover and bake at the same temperature called for in the original recipe. Bake until it is heated through. Or, place the frozen food on a non-metal serving dish. Cover and microwave until heated through, following directions in your microwave manual for reheating frozen entrees.

A Saturday-Night Dinner For Two

Creamy Baked Chicken, below
Salad of Three Greens & Four Vegetables
Herb Vinaigrette
Casserole Biscuits, page 19, Butter
Grapes, Cream Cheese
Pinot Chardonnay
Irish Coffee

◆

Make-Ahead Dinner For Two

Beef & Mushrooms, page 91
Feathered Rice, page 88
Marinated-Vegetable Salad
Rye Rolls, Butter
Raspberry Sorbet with Cookies
Cabernet Sauvignon
Coffee

Creamy Baked Chicken

Today's tender chicken cooks quickly but often needs a flavor boost.

2 chicken legs and thighs, split (4 pieces)
1/2 teaspoon salt
1/4 teaspoon pepper
Dash of paprika
1 tablespoon butter
1 teaspoon all-purpose flour
1 teaspoon Dijon-style mustard
1/4 cup dry white wine

1/4 cup chicken broth
1/4 cup whipping cream
1 cup sliced fresh mushrooms
1/4 cup sliced, stuffed, green olives
2 tablespoons minced fresh parsley
1 teaspoon fines herbes or
  Herbes de Provence
1/4 cup chopped salted sunflower kernels

Preheat oven to 375F (190C). Wash chicken; pat dry with paper towels. Sprinkle with salt, pepper and paprika. In a large heavy skillet, melt butter. Add chicken and brown thoroughly on both sides; remove to a 1-quart casserole. Stir flour and mustard into chicken drippings in skillet. Whisk in wine, broth and cream; bring to a boil, whisking constantly, about 3 minutes or until sauce is thickened. Stir in mushrooms, olives, parsley and herbs. Pour sauce over chicken in casserole. Bake, covered, 30 minutes or until chicken is tender. Sprinkle with sunflower kernels. Bake, uncovered, 5 minutes longer. Makes 2 servings.

Individual Chicken Pot Pies

You'll love using cooked chicken this way!

Mock Puff Pastry, page 36
1 tablespoon butter
4 medium, fresh mushrooms, quartered
4 bulb ends of green onions, chopped
2 tablespoons all-purpose flour
1 cup chicken broth
1 teaspoon Worcestershire sauce

1 cup fresh or frozen green peas
1 tablespoon chopped pimento, if desired
1 egg yolk
1/4 cup half and half
1-1/2 cups diced cooked chicken or turkey
Salt and pepper to taste
Milk

Prepare dough for Mock Puff Pastry; wrap and refrigerate. Preheat oven to 425F (220C). In a large skillet, melt butter. Add mushrooms and green onions; sauté about 4 minutes or until onions are soft. Sprinkle with flour; stir until blended. Stir in broth, Worcestershire sauce, peas and pimento, if desired. In a small bowl, combine egg yolk and half and half. Stir into mushroom mixture along with chicken or turkey. Cook over low heat until heated through. Season with salt and pepper, if necessary. Divide mixture between 2 (1-1/2-cup) individual casseroles. On a pastry cloth or lightly floured board, roll out chilled dough to make an 1/8-inch-thick rectangle. Roll up jelly-roll fashion and roll out again to a rectangle. Fold from long ends over the center to make a square of dough. Roll out and cut dough to fit over filling in each casserole. Reserve dough scraps for decoration. Place rolled dough over filling in each casserole; seal dough to edge. Pierce dough with a fork to make vent holes or cut out small shapes. If desired, roll and cut reserved dough scraps into decorative shapes; place on pies. Brush top of dough with milk. Bake 20 to 30 minutes or until pastry is crisp and golden. Makes 2 servings.

Feathered Rice

This goes well with simmered meats or barbecued steak or chicken.

1/2 cup uncooked extra-long-grain or
    regular long-grain white rice
2 tablespoons butter
1/2 cup sliced fresh mushrooms

4 green onions, sliced
1-1/4 cups chicken broth or water
Salt to taste, if not using chicken broth

Preheat oven to 300F (150C). Butter a 1-quart casserole. Spread rice on a baking sheet; toast in oven, uncovered, 20 to 30 minutes or until golden. While rice toasts, melt butter in a medium, heavy skillet. Add mushrooms and green onions; sauté 5 minutes or until tender but not browned. Remove toasted rice to buttered casserole. Add mushrooms, green onions, chicken broth or water, and salt, if used; stir. Bake, covered, 35 to 45 minutes or until rice is tender and has absorbed all the liquid. Before serving, fluff with a fork. Makes 2 servings.

Individual Chicken Pot Pies

Country Ham Pies

To save calories, use turkey ham in place of regular ham.

2 tablespoons butter
2 tablespoons chopped green onion
2 tablespoons all-purpose flour
1/8 teaspoon rubbed sage
1 teaspoon chicken bouillon granules or
   1 bouillon cube
2/3 cup milk

1/2 cup water
1 cup cubed cooked ham or turkey ham
1/2 cup cooked frozen mixed vegetables,
   drained
1 tablespoon chopped fresh parsley
1 (6-oz.) pkg. refrigerated biscuit dough

Preheat oven to 400F (205C). Butter 2 (1-1/2-cup) individual casseroles. In a small skillet, melt butter. Add green onion; sauté until tender but not browned. Stir in flour, sage and bouillon granules or cube until blended. Whisk in milk and water; bring to a boil, whisking constantly, until thickened and bubbly. Stir in ham, vegetables and parsley; heat until mixture bubbles. Spoon into buttered casseroles. Cut each of 2 biscuits into 4 portions. Arrange 4 biscuit portions over mixture in each casserole. Place casseroles on a baking sheet; arrange remaining biscuits next to casseroles. Bake 10 to 15 minutes or until biscuits are golden. Makes 2 servings.

French Egg Casserole

This is a great way to use up extra hard-cooked eggs from the Easter bunny!

1 slice leftover buttered toast
4 hard-cooked eggs
Herbed White Sauce, see below

4 bacon slices, crisp-cooked, crumbled
1 cup shredded sharp Cheddar cheese (4 oz.)

Herbed White Sauce:
2 tablespoons butter
2 tablespoons all-purpose flour
1/4 teaspoon salt
1 cup milk

1 tablespoon chopped fresh parsley
1/8 teaspoon dried leaf thyme
1/8 teaspoon dried leaf marjoram
1/8 teaspoon dried leaf basil

Preheat oven to 350F (175C). In a food processor fitted with a steel blade, process buttered toast until fine crumbs; set aside. Cut eggs into thin slices. Prepare Herbed White Sauce. Spoon 2 tablespoons sauce into each of 2 (1-1/2-cup) individual casseroles. Add a layer of egg slices, then a few bacon pieces, then more sauce. Continue layering until ingredients are used up, ending with sauce. Sprinkle with cheese and buttered crumbs. Bake, uncovered, 15 minutes or until bubbly and crumbs are browned. Makes 2 servings.

Herbed White Sauce:

In a medium saucepan, melt butter. Stir in flour and salt until smooth. Cook, stirring constantly, over medium heat 2 minutes. Whisk in milk; bring to a boil, whisking constantly until thickened and smooth. Stir in parsley, thyme, marjoram and basil. Makes about 1 cup.

How to Make Country Ham Pies

1/Spoon ham mixture into individual casseroles. Cut each of 2 biscuits into 4 portions.

2/Arrange 4 biscuit portions over mixture in each casserole. Place on a baking sheet; arrange remaining biscuits next to casseroles. Bake until biscuits are golden.

Beef & Mushrooms

You can prepare most of this a day ahead.

2 tablespoons butter
1 lb. beef tenderloin tips or
   beef minute steaks
8 oz. fresh mushroom caps

1/2 cup chopped green onion,
   including tops
1/2 cup dry white wine
1 teaspoon salt

Butter a shallow 1-quart casserole. In a large skillet, melt 1 tablespoon butter. Add meat; brown quickly on both sides. Remove to buttered casserole. In same skillet, melt remaining butter. Add mushroom caps; sauté quickly until browned. Arrange on top of meat. Add green onion to skillet; sauté about 5 minutes or until tender but not browned. Add to mushrooms and meat in casserole. Pour wine into skillet and bring to a boil, stirring constantly to scrape up meat drippings. Boil until reduced by half; pour over meat and vegetables in casserole. Sprinkle with salt. Preheat oven to 400F (205C). Bake, uncovered, 10 to 15 minutes for medium-rare or until cooked to your liking. Meat will be well-done if baked 30 minutes. Makes 2 servings.

Budget Casseroles

Casseroles can be great budget-stretchers. The peasant food of almost any country has created lots of good-tasting combinations which we can easily adapt to our ingredients and lifestyles. A wise cook needs only to look around the world for ideas.

Depending on which area of the world the original dish came from, meat and vegetable protein are combined in different ways. Northern Europeans and Scandinavians often use meat and potatoes in the same dish. Mexican and Spanish foods frequently stretch meat with corn or beans.

Whether you choose exotic or familiar casseroles will depend on your mood, the ingredients on hand and perhaps the age group you are serving. Young people tend to accept Mexican and Italian ideas readily, although some would not enjoy the spicy flavor. In fact, the amount of "heat" in a dish can easily be controlled. As many of our older population travel, there is a greater interest than before in sampling and cooking ethnic foods.

You might try this fun and economical Mexican-style menu for young or old. The menu combines the proteins of cheese, corn and ground beef.

Mexican-Style Buffet

Tortilla Chips, Salsa
Mexican Enchiladas, page 98
Baked Chilies Rellenos, page 134
Salad of Romaine, Tomato, Onion & Cucumber
Caper Vinaigrette
Fresh-Fruit Platter
Mexican Beer
Coffee

Oriental Beef & Mushrooms

A family with a hectic dinner schedule will enjoy this one!

1 lb. extra-lean ground beef
2 large onions, halved, sliced lengthwise
1 large garlic clove, minced, if desired
2 cups sliced celery, cut diagonally
   in 1/2-inch pieces
8 oz. fresh mushrooms, sliced
1 (12-oz.) pkg. fresh bean sprouts

1 (8-oz.) can sliced water chestnuts,
   drained
1 (16-oz.) can sliced tomatoes
2 tablespoons cornstarch
2 tablespoons soy sauce
2 cups chow-mein noodles
Hot cooked rice

Preheat oven to 350F (175C). In a large skillet, cook beef until crumbly and no longer pink. Turn into a 2-1/2-quart casserole, reserving drippings in skillet. Add onions, garlic, celery and mushrooms to drippings in skillet; sauté until crisp-tender. Add to meat in casserole. Fold in bean sprouts, water chestnuts and tomatoes with juice. In a small bowl, blend cornstarch and soy sauce; stir into meat mixture. Top with chow-mein noodles. Bake, uncovered, 45 minutes to 1 hour or until juices are thickened and clear. Serve with hot cooked rice. Makes 6 servings.

Meat, Eggplant & Mozzarella Casserole

Serve antipasto salad and crisp breadsticks with this tasty dish.

Meat Sauce, see below
1 medium eggplant, cut in 1/2-inch slices
All-purpose flour
1 egg

2 tablespoons water
Oil for deep-frying
4 cups shredded mozzarella cheese (1 lb.)
1/2 cup grated Parmesan cheese (1-1/2 oz.)

Meat Sauce:
1 lb. extra-lean ground beef
1 lb. fresh Italian sausage
1 green bell pepper, minced
2 medium onions, chopped

8 oz. fresh mushrooms, chopped
1 (15-oz.) can tomato sauce
1 (16-oz.) can tomatoes

Prepare Meat Sauce; set aside. Coat eggplant slices with flour. In a medium, shallow dish, beat egg and water. Dip eggplant slices in egg mixture, then again in flour. In a large heavy skillet, pour oil to a depth of 1/4 inch; heat oil over medium heat until eggplant sizzles when added. Brown coated eggplant slices on both sides. Drain on paper towels. Preheat oven to 375F (190C). Butter a 3-quart casserole. In a medium bowl, toss cheeses together until blended; set aside. Arrange 1/2 of browned eggplant slices over bottom of buttered casserole. Top with 1/2 of Meat Sauce, then sprinkle with 1/2 of cheese mixture. Top with remaining eggplant, remaining sauce and remaining cheese mixture. Bake, uncovered, 40 to 50 minutes or until bubbly and cheese is lightly browned. Makes 8 servings.

Meat Sauce:
Crumble beef and sausage into a large skillet. Add green pepper, onions and mushrooms. Cook until meat is crumbly and no longer pink. Add tomato sauce and tomatoes with juice; simmer 45 minutes. Skim off fat. Makes about 8 cups.

Spinach-Stuffed Meat Squares

Spinach and cheese are sandwiched between the meat in this flavorful dish.

1 lb. fresh spinach or 1 (10-oz.) pkg.
  frozen chopped spinach
1 cup shredded mozzarella or
  Monterey Jack cheese (4 oz.)
1 lb. extra-lean ground beef
3/4 cup regular or quick-cooking rolled oats

2/3 cup ketchup
1 egg, beaten
1/4 cup chopped onion
1 teaspoon garlic salt
1 teaspoon dried leaf oregano
1/2 teaspoon dried leaf basil

Preheat oven to 350F (175C). Cook spinach; drain well. Press spinach in a sieve to remove excess liquid. In a small bowl, mix spinach and 1/2 cup cheese; set aside. In a large bowl, thoroughly combine beef, oats, ketchup, egg, onion, garlic salt, oregano and basil. Press 1/2 of meat mixture into an 8-inch-square baking dish. Top with spinach mixture in an even layer, then remaining meat mixture in an even layer. Bake, uncovered, 30 to 45 minutes or until meat shrinks away from sides of dish. Drain off any extra fat from baking dish; sprinkle with remaining cheese. Bake, uncovered, 5 minutes longer or until cheese is melted. Let stand 10 minutes before cutting into 6 squares. Makes 6 servings.

Great Northern Beans & Bacon

Economical and great tasting; the Garlic-Crumb Topping does it!

1 (16-oz.) pkg. Great Northern beans or
  dried white beans
2 qts. water
1 tablespoon salt
8 oz. thick-sliced bacon, diced

1 medium carrot, shredded
2 bunches green onions, chopped
1 teaspoon dried leaf thyme
1 cup white wine
Garlic-Crumb Topping, see below

Garlic-Crumb Topping:
1 cup dry breadcrumbs
1/2 cup chopped fresh parsley

2 garlic cloves, minced
1/4 cup butter, melted

Wash beans and pick over. Place in a large bowl; add water to cover. Soak overnight; drain. Place in a large saucepan with 2 quarts water and salt. Bring to a boil; reduce heat and simmer 20 minutes. While beans cook, sauté bacon in a medium, heavy skillet 5 minutes or until skillet is coated with fat. Add carrot and green onions; sauté 10 minutes. Turn into a 2-quart casserole. Stir in thyme, wine and beans with cooking liquid. Bake, covered, in a 300F (150C) oven 3 hours. Stir occasionally. If beans are watery, uncover and bake 30 minutes longer. Prepare Garlic-Crumb Topping; sprinkle over beans. Preheat broiler; broil 6 inches from heat until topping is browned. Makes 8 servings.

Garlic-Crumb Topping:
In a small bowl, combine all ingredients until breadcrumbs are evenly coated with butter.

How to Make Spinach-Stuffed Meat Squares

1/Press 1/2 of meat mixture into an 8-inch-square baking dish.

2/Top meat mixture with spinach mixture in an even layer, then remaining meat mixture.

Shepherd's Pie

This is a delicious way to use leftover cooked meat and gravy.

3 cups ground cooked meat
1/2 cup minced onion
2/3 cup leftover meat gravy or brown sauce
1/4 cup minced fresh parsley
1/4 cup minced celery
1/4 teaspoon rubbed sage

Salt and pepper to taste
3 cups mashed potatoes
   (3 or 4 large potatoes)
1/4 cup butter
1/4 cup shredded cheese, Cheddar, Swiss,
   Monterey Jack or mozzarella (1 oz.)

Preheat oven to 400F (205C). Butter a shallow 1-1/2-quart casserole or 8-inch-square baking dish. In a large bowl, thoroughly combine meat, onion, gravy or sauce, parsley, celery, sage, salt and pepper. Turn into buttered casserole. Smooth mashed potatoes in an even layer over top of meat mixture. Dot with butter; sprinkle with cheese. Bake, uncovered, 35 to 40 minutes or until heated through and top is browned. Makes 6 servings.

Variations
You can add leftover cooked vegetables, sautéed mushrooms, or use any combination of cooked meat in this dish.

Meat-Filled Crepes

For a party, triple this recipe to serve more than 20!

Crepes, see below
1 (10-oz.) pkg. frozen chopped spinach,
   cooked, drained
8 oz. extra-lean ground beef
4 oz. fresh Italian sausage
1 garlic clove, minced

1/2 teaspoon dried leaf oregano
1/2 teaspoon dried leaf basil
Salt to taste
1 (15-oz.) can tomato sauce
3/4 cup shredded cheese, white Cheddar,
   Monterey Jack or mozzarella (3 oz.)

Crepes:
3 eggs
1/2 cup all-purpose flour
1/4 teaspoon salt

1 cup milk
Butter to cook crepes

Prepare Crepes; set aside. Preheat oven to 350F (175C). Butter a 13" x 9" baking dish. Press spinach in a sieve to remove excess liquid. In a large skillet, cook beef, sausage and garlic until meat is crumbly and no longer pink. Stir in spinach, oregano, basil and salt; cool slightly. Divide mixture between crepes and roll up. Arrange, seam-side down, in a single layer in buttered baking dish. Pour tomato sauce over filled crepes. Sprinkle with cheese. Bake, uncovered, 30 minutes or until bubbly. Makes 6 servings.

Crepes:
In a medium bowl, whisk eggs, flour, salt and milk. Strain batter into another medium bowl; cover and refrigerate 30 minutes. To make crepes, heat an 8-inch crepe or omelet pan until a drop of water sizzles on it. Lightly butter pan. Ladle about 2 tablespoons batter into pan and swirl to coat surface thinly. When browned on 1 side, remove. Stack crepes as they are cooked. Repeat with remaining batter, adding butter to pan as needed. Makes 12 crepes.

Swiss Meatballs in Wine & Cheese Sauce

If you make the meatballs tiny, they are great for appetizers!

1 lb. lean ground pork
1 lb. ground cooked ham
1-1/4 cups dry breadcrumbs
1/2 cup milk
1 egg
1 medium onion, minced
1 teaspoon dried leaf marjoram

1 teaspoon salt
1/4 teaspoon pepper
1 cup white wine
1 cup water
1-1/2 tablespoons cornstarch
2 cups shredded Swiss cheese (8 oz.)

Preheat oven to 350F (175C). Lightly butter a shallow 2-quart casserole or 8-inch-square baking dish. In a large bowl, thoroughly combine pork, ham, breadcrumbs, milk, egg, onion, marjoram, salt and pepper. Shape into walnut-sized balls. Place in a single layer in buttered casserole. Pour wine and 3/4 cup water over meatballs. Bake, uncovered, 45 minutes or until cooked through. Drain casserole juices into a medium skillet. Bring to a boil. In a small bowl, blend cornstarch and remaining 1/4 cup water; stir into boiling juices. Cook, stirring constantly, until thickened and clear. Pour over meatballs. Sprinkle with cheese. Return to 350F (175C) oven and bake, uncovered, about 5 minutes longer or until cheese is melted. Makes 8 servings.

Tamale Pie   *Photo on page 99.*

A delicious corn-bread topping gives this casserole extra appeal.

2 tablespoons vegetable oil
1 cup chopped onion
1 cup chopped green bell pepper
1 lb. extra-lean ground beef
1 (14- to 15-oz.) can tomato wedges
  in tomato sauce
2 tablespoons tomato paste
1 (10-oz.) pkg. thawed, frozen,
  whole-kernel corn

1 cup sliced, stuffed, green olives
1 tablespoon ground cumin
2 teaspoons unsweetened cocoa powder
1-1/2 teaspoons salt
1/2 teaspoon ground allspice
2 teaspoons chili powder
1/4 to 1 teaspoon hot-pepper sauce
1 tablespoon yellow cornmeal
Tamale Topping, see below

Tamale Topping:
1 cup all-purpose flour
1 cup yellow cornmeal
3 tablespoons sugar
2 teaspoons baking powder
3 tablespoons butter, melted

3/4 cup milk
1 large egg, slightly beaten
1/2 cup shredded sharp Cheddar cheese
  (2 oz.)
1 (4-oz.) can diced green chilies

In a large skillet, heat oil. Add onion and green pepper; sauté until tender. Add beef; cook until crumbly and no longer pink. Add tomatoes, tomato paste, corn, olives, cumin, cocoa powder, salt, allspice, chili powder, pepper sauce and cornmeal. Simmer, stirring frequently, 30 minutes. Spoon into a shallow 2-1/2-quart casserole. Preheat oven to 400F (205C). Prepare Tamale Topping. Spoon topping in large spoonfuls around edge of casserole. Bake, uncovered, 10 minutes. Reduce heat to 350F (175C); bake, uncovered, 30 minutes longer or until cornmeal topping is cooked through and lightly browned. Makes 8 servings.

Tamale Topping:
In a large bowl, mix flour, cornmeal, sugar and baking powder. Add butter, milk and egg, stirring until dry ingredients are just moistened. Quickly stir in cheese and chilies.

Four-Bean Beef Bake

Quick to make if you have a well-stocked pantry and ground beef!

8 oz. bacon slices, diced
1 lb. extra-lean ground beef
1/2 cup chopped onion
2 tablespoons brown sugar
1 teaspoon salt
1/2 cup ketchup

1 tablespoon prepared mustard
1 (16-oz.) can pork and beans
1 (16-oz.) can kidney beans, drained
1 (16-oz.) can butter beans, drained
1 (16-oz.) can lima beans, drained

Preheat oven to 350F (175C). In a large skillet, cook bacon until crisp; drain off fat. Add beef and cook until crumbly and no longer pink; drain off fat. Add onion; cook 2 minutes longer. In a 2-1/2-quart casserole, combine beef mixture and remaining ingredients. Bake, uncovered, 30 minutes or until heated through and bubbly. Makes 8 servings.

Mexican Enchiladas

Casserole-style enchiladas are easy to serve.

1 lb. extra-lean ground beef	2 tablespoons all-purpose flour
1 medium onion, chopped	2 (8-oz.) cans tomato sauce
3 garlic cloves, minced	1 cup beef broth
1 tablespoon red-wine vinegar	2 cups shredded sharp Cheddar cheese
1 to 2 tablespoons chili powder	(8 oz.)
1 teaspoon salt	12 (6-inch) corn tortillas
1/2 teaspoon dried leaf oregano	2 green onions, sliced
1 (4-oz.) can sliced black olives	Guacamole, if desired

In a large heavy skillet, cook beef, onion and garlic over medium heat 7 to 10 minutes or until meat is crumbly and no longer pink. Stir in vinegar, chili powder, salt, oregano, olives and flour until blended. Stir in 1 can tomato sauce and 1/2 of beef broth. Cook, stirring constantly, 20 minutes or until meat mixture is thick. Add 1/2 of cheese to meat mixture; set aside. In a small bowl, blend remaining can tomato sauce with remaining beef broth; set aside. To soften tortillas, wrap in paper towels; place in a microwave oven. Microwave at full power (HIGH) 1 minute or until just warmed. Or, wrap in foil and place in a 300F (150C) oven 10 minutes or until just warmed. Butter a 13" x 9" baking dish. Preheat oven to 350F (175C). Divide meat mixture between 12 tortillas and roll up. Arrange, seam-side down, in a single layer in buttered baking dish. Pour tomato-sauce mixture over tortillas; sprinkle with green onions and remaining cheese. Bake, uncovered, 35 minutes or until heated through. Serve with guacamole, if desired. Makes 6 servings.

Chili Oven Pancake

This is a puffy oven pancake with a beef-chili filling.

1 lb. extra-lean ground beef	1 small green bell pepper, diced
1 small onion, chopped	1 teaspoon salt
1 garlic clove, minced	1 cup cubed Monterey Jack cheese
2 teaspoons chili powder	(about 4 oz.)
1 teaspoon ground cumin	2 eggs
1 teaspoon dried leaf oregano	1 cup all-purpose flour
1 (4-oz.) can diced green chilies, drained	1 cup milk
1 (12-oz.) can whole-kernel corn, drained	1/2 teaspoon salt

Preheat oven to 400F (205C). Place a shallow 1-1/2-quart casserole in oven while it preheats. In a large skillet, cook meat until crumbly and no longer pink; drain off all but 2 tablespoons fat. Add onion, garlic, chili powder, cumin, oregano and chilies to skillet. Cook, stirring constantly, until onion is tender. Stir in corn, green pepper and salt. Turn into hot casserole; sprinkle with cheese. In a medium bowl, beat eggs, flour, milk and salt until smooth. Spoon batter over top of meat mixture in casserole. Bake, uncovered, 25 minutes or until puffy and well-browned. Makes 6 servings.

Clockwise from the top: Mexican Enchiladas, above; Tamale Pie, page 97; and Baked Tacos, page 101.

Brazilian Feijoada

Manioc flour is made from the root of cassava and can be found in health-food stores.

2 cups dried black beans
1 teaspoon salt
1/2 teaspoon pepper
2 garlic cloves, minced
1/4 cup diced salt pork (about 2 oz.)
1 (1-lb.) ham shank

1 (28-oz.) can whole tomatoes
1 medium onion, chopped
4 cups water
12 oz. linguiça or Spanish chorizo, sliced
Buttered Manioc, see below
Hot cooked rice

Buttered Manioc:
1 tablespoon butter
1 cup manioc flour, regular farina, or
    regular or instant Cream of Wheat
1/2 cup chopped fresh parsley

1/2 cup raisins
1/2 cup sliced, stuffed, green olives
1/2 cup diced cooked ham

Wash beans and pick over. Place in a 2- to 3-quart casserole; add water to cover. Soak overnight; drain. Stir in salt, pepper, garlic, salt pork, ham shank, tomatoes with juice, onion and 4 cups water. Bake, covered, in a 325F (165C) oven 4 hours. Check occasionally, adding more water to keep mixture moist, if necessary. Remove cover and stir in sausage. Bake, uncovered, 30 to 45 minutes longer or until liquid is thickened and sausage is browned. Prepare Buttered Manioc. Serve casserole with Buttered Manioc to sprinkle over top of each serving, and hot cooked rice. Makes 6 to 8 servings.

Buttered Manioc:
In a medium skillet, melt butter. Add manioc flour, farina or Cream of Wheat; stir over medium-low heat so grains stay loose and dry and become light golden. Grains should absorb butter flavor. Stir in parsley, raisins, olives and ham. Serve at room temperature. Refrigerate any left-over Buttered Manioc.

To soak beans quickly, pour cold water to cover over washed beans. Boil 2 minutes, then remove from heat. Let beans stand, covered, 1 hour.

How to Make Brazilian Feijoada

1/Stir parsley, raisins, olives and ham into buttered manioc flour.

2/Serve Brazilian Feijoada with Buttered Manioc sprinkled over the top, and hot cooked rice.

Baked Tacos   Photo on page 99.

Easy tacos are a favorite with children.

12 crisp taco shells or 12 (6-inch) corn tortillas and oil for deep-frying	1 teaspoon salt
2 tablespoons vegetable oil	1 (8-oz.) can tomatoes
1 small onion, chopped	4 cups shredded Monterey Jack cheese (1 lb.)
12 oz. extra-lean ground beef	1 pint dairy sour cream (2 cups)
1 teaspoon dried leaf oregano	Shredded iceberg lettuce
2 tablespoons green taco sauce, jalapeño sauce or chili relish	Diced or wedged fresh tomatoes

Arrange taco shells, open-side up, in a 13'' x 9'' baking dish. If using soft tortillas, pour oil to a depth of 1/2 inch in a large heavy skillet or deep-fryer. Heat oil to 365F (185C) or until a 1-inch cube of bread turns golden brown in 60 seconds. Dip a tortilla in hot oil on both sides to soften it. Holding it with tongs, fold softened tortilla into a U shape and fry until crisp, turning once. Repeat with remaining tortillas. Drain on paper towels; cool. Place, open-side up, in baking dish. Preheat oven to 325F (165C). In a large skillet, heat 2 tablespoons oil. Add onion; sauté about 5 minutes or until tender. Add beef; cook until crumbly and no longer pink, but not dry. Add oregano, taco sauce or relish, salt and tomatoes with juice, breaking up tomatoes with a spoon. Using 1/2 of meat mixture, spoon some into each taco shell. Sprinkle 1/2 of cheese over meat mixture in tacos. Top with remaining meat mixture, then with remaining cheese. Bake, uncovered, 25 to 30 minutes or until heated through. Garnish with sour cream, lettuce and tomatoes. Makes 6 to 12 servings.

Quantity Cooking

What do you consider *quantity cooking?* To cook for 12 is quantity to one person and normal to another. Well then, is it 20 or 25? In this chapter I have covered this range by including recipes that serve from 12 to 25 people.

For a full-scale family gathering or family reunion, I suggest preparing more than one of the casseroles, or making a double batch of one of them twice. Most home kitchens do not have casserole dishes large enough to handle extra-large quantities, and smaller quantities are easier to manage for cooking and storage.

For instance, if you plan to have a crowd of 100 guests, find a casserole recipe that serves 10 to 12, and make it 8 to 10 times. If you make a single recipe several times, it is easier to figure out the number of servings. Alternatively, you may choose to serve several different kinds of casseroles. When there is a greater variety of foods, people tend to eat more, selecting from many different dishes. You should figure on a total number of servings 25 to 35 percent greater than the number of guests.

Here is an efficient "plan of action" to help you with your next large party:

1. Select recipes for casseroles which can be easily prepared in advance. Most casseroles in this book and all the recipes in this chapter can be made ahead.

2. Read through the recipe ahead of time, noting everything that must be purchased or borrowed. You may need to borrow baking dishes or casseroles.

3. To save money, purchase ingredients in as large quantities as possible without overbuying.

4. Get all the ingredients ready as listed in the recipe ingredient list and method. For instance, chop onions, mince garlic and brown ground beef. Sometimes this preparation can be done a day ahead of the assembly and the actual assembly done the day before a party.

5. Do all similar operations at one time. For instance, if the recipe calls for 1 cup chopped onion, chop the onion for all eight or ten recipes at one time. Wherever possible, use a food processor for tedious work such as chopping, slicing and shredding.

6. When all ingredients are ready for assembly, line up the casserole dishes. For maximum

efficiency, the dishes should all be the same size and shape. Casseroles that vary in depth and size may require slightly different baking times and more attention from the cook.

A word about food safety: When preparing large quantities of food, the chances for food contamination are multiplied. Large quantities of food, such as meats, sauces and cheeses, tend to be harder to cool down.

Bacteria which can contaminate food and make people sick, grow in food at temperatures between 45F and 140F. During incubation, bacteria do not multiply, they divide. They divide every twenty minutes causing an enormous mathematical progression in numbers. Because of this progression, food-sanitation officials recommend that any potentially hazardous ingredient not be held in the critical temperature zone for more than two hours. The basic rule is to keep hot foods hot (over 140F), and cold foods cold (under 45F).

Which are "potentially hazardous" foods? Any non-acid, creamy, moist food with starch or protein ingredients, such as sauces and custards, and mixtures containing meats, poultry, fish or egg. Baked goods, such as breads and unfilled cakes and pastries, can be held at room temperature without problems. Fresh fruits and vegetables can be held at room temperature, but are often more palatable when served crisp and cold from the refrigerator.

For ultimate convenience, all of these casseroles can be prepared ahead of the party date and baked just before serving.

Below are menu suggestions for 25 and 50 guests.

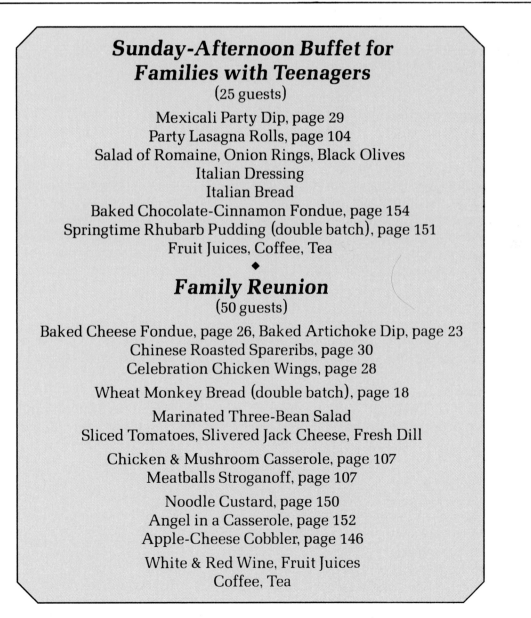

Sunday-Afternoon Buffet for Families with Teenagers
(25 guests)

Mexicali Party Dip, page 29
Party Lasagna Rolls, page 104
Salad of Romaine, Onion Rings, Black Olives
Italian Dressing
Italian Bread
Baked Chocolate-Cinnamon Fondue, page 154
Springtime Rhubarb Pudding (double batch), page 151
Fruit Juices, Coffee, Tea

◆

Family Reunion
(50 guests)

Baked Cheese Fondue, page 26, Baked Artichoke Dip, page 23
Chinese Roasted Spareribs, page 30
Celebration Chicken Wings, page 28

Wheat Monkey Bread (double batch), page 18

Marinated Three-Bean Salad
Sliced Tomatoes, Slivered Jack Cheese, Fresh Dill

Chicken & Mushroom Casserole, page 107
Meatballs Stroganoff, page 107

Noodle Custard, page 150
Angel in a Casserole, page 152
Apple-Cheese Cobbler, page 146

White & Red Wine, Fruit Juices
Coffee, Tea

Party Lasagna Rolls

Prepare the parts to this dish a day in advance.

1/2 cup butter
2 large onions, chopped
2 garlic cloves, minced
1-1/4 lbs. extra-lean ground beef
1 lb. ground turkey, or 8 oz. each
   lean ground pork and ground veal
16 oz. ricotta or cream-style cottage cheese
   (2 cups)
1 cup grated Parmesan cheese (3 oz.)

4 egg yolks
Salt to taste
1/4 teaspoon ground nutmeg
1/2 cup chopped fresh parsley
White Sauce, see below
Herbed Tomato Sauce, see below
2 (1-lb.) pkgs. lasagna noodles
3 lbs. mozzarella cheese or
   Monterey Jack cheese, sliced

White Sauce:
1/4 cup butter
1/3 cup all-purpose flour

1 pint hot milk (2 cups)
3 cups hot chicken broth

Herbed Tomato Sauce:
3 tablespoons butter
1/4 cup chopped green onion
2 (15-oz.) cans tomato sauce

1 cup chicken broth
1 teaspoon dried leaf basil
1/2 teaspoon salt

In a large skillet, melt butter. Add onions and garlic; sauté 10 minutes or until onions are very tender. Add ground meats; sauté until crumbly and no longer pink. Drain off fat. Place meat mixture in a large bowl; cool. Stir in ricotta or cottage cheese, Parmesan cheese, egg yolks, salt, nutmeg and parsley; mix well. Set aside. Prepare White Sauce and Herbed Tomato Sauce; set aside. To assemble casserole, spoon 1/2 of each sauce into bottom of 2 (13" x 9") pans or 1 (15" x 10") jelly-roll pan. Cook lasagna noodles according to package directions until tender but firm to the bite; drain. To prevent sticking, lay noodles in a shallow dish with cold water to cover; add 1 teaspoon vegetable oil. Preheat oven to 375F (190C). Lay noodles out flat. Divide meat mixture between noodles; spread over 2/3 of each noodle. Roll up. Stand up filled rolls close together in sauced pans. Spoon remaining White Sauce and Tomato Sauce over rolls. Top with sliced cheese. Bake, uncovered, 45 minutes to 1 hour or until heated through and cheese is melted. Makes 20 to 24 servings.

White Sauce:
In a medium saucepan, melt butter. Stir in flour until smooth. Whisk in hot milk and hot chicken broth. Bring to a boil, whisking constantly until thickened and smooth; cool. Makes 5 cups.

Herbed Tomato Sauce:
In a large skillet, melt butter. Add green onion; sauté 2 to 3 minutes or until soft. Add tomato sauce, chicken broth, basil and salt. Simmer, uncovered, 30 minutes or until reduced and slightly thickened; cool. Makes 5 cups.

How to Make Party Lasagna Rolls

1/Spoon 1/2 of each sauce into bottom of lasagna pans. Divide meat mixture between cooked lasagna noodles; spread over 2/3 of each noodle. Roll up.

2/Stand up filled rolls close together in sauced pans. Spoon remaining White Sauce and Herbed Tomato Sauce over rolls. Top with sliced cheese. Bake until heated through and cheese is melted.

Choucroute Garni

Literally translated, this means garnished cabbage!

2 (1-lb. 13-oz.) cans sauerkraut,
   rinsed, squeezed dry
2 large Golden Delicious apples,
   peeled, cored, sliced
4 bacon slices, diced
6 black peppercorns
6 juniper berries

1 cup dry white wine
12 smoked pork chops or 2 lbs. smoked ham,
   cut in 1/2-inch slices
12 garlic-flavored smoked-sausage links
   (about 3 lbs.)
1/4 cup chopped fresh parsley

In a wide 5-quart casserole, combine sauerkraut, apples, bacon, peppercorns, juniper berries and wine. Spread evenly in casserole. Bake, covered, in a 300F (150C) oven 2-1/2 hours. Arrange pork chops or ham on top. Bake, covered, 30 minutes longer. Cut sausages diagonally into 3-inch slices. Tuck sausage slices into sauerkraut mixture. Bake, covered, 30 minutes longer or until sausages are heated through. To serve, spoon sauerkraut onto a rimmed platter; arrange meat and sausages over sauerkraut. Garnish with parsley. Makes 12 generous servings.

Mock Ravioli

An old favorite that tastes like ravioli.

1 (16-oz.) pkg. large macaroni shells
Spinach Filling, see below
Meat Filling, see below
1/2 pint dairy sour cream (1 cup)

1/2 cup grated Parmesan cheese
  (1-1/2 oz.)
1 cup shredded mozzarella cheese (4 oz.)

Spinach Filling:
2 (10-oz.) pkgs. thawed, frozen,
  chopped spinach, drained
1/4 cup vegetable oil
2 cups fresh breadcrumbs
1/2 cup minced fresh parsley

1/2 cup grated Parmesan cheese (1-1/2 oz.)
1 teaspoon rubbed sage
1 teaspoon salt
1/2 teaspoon ground nutmeg

Meat Filling:
1 lb. extra-lean ground beef
1 lb. fresh Italian sausage
2 medium onions, chopped
1 garlic clove, minced
8 oz. fresh mushrooms, sliced
1 (8-oz.) can tomato sauce
1 (6-oz.) can tomato paste

1 cup water
1/2 teaspoon dried leaf oregano
1/2 teaspoon dried leaf basil
1/2 teaspoon dried leaf thyme
1 teaspoon salt
1/2 teaspoon pepper

Butter a shallow 3-quart casserole or 13" x 9" baking dish. Cook macaroni according to package directions until tender but firm to the bite; drain. Rinse with cold water to prevent sticking; drain well. Prepare Spinach Filling. Prepare Meat Filling. Preheat oven to 350F (175C). Layer 1/2 of macaroni in bottom of buttered casserole. Top with 1/2 of Spinach Filling, then 1/2 of Meat Filling. Repeat layers ending with Meat Filling. In a small bowl, blend sour cream and Parmesan cheese; dot over top of meat layer in casserole. Sprinkle with mozzarella cheese. Bake, uncovered, 30 minutes or until heated through and cheese is melted. Makes 12 servings.

Spinach Filling:
Press spinach in a sieve to remove excess liquid. In a large bowl, thoroughly combine oil, spinach, breadcrumbs, parsley, Parmesan cheese, sage, salt and nutmeg.

Meat Filling:
In a large skillet, sauté beef, sausage, onions and garlic until meat is crumbly and no longer pink. Add mushrooms, tomato sauce, tomato paste, water, herbs, salt and pepper; stir to blend. Cover and simmer 1-1/2 hours, stirring occasionally.

Use a # 70 ice-cream scoop to shape meatballs easily.

Chicken & Mushroom Casserole

Serve this festive casserole with Easy Rice & Tomato Pilaf, page 138, and Caesar salad.

6 (3-lb.) chickens, each cut into
   8 serving pieces
2 tablespoons salt
2 teaspoons pepper
2 teaspoons paprika
1 cup butter

2 lbs. fresh mushrooms, sliced
1/2 cup all-purpose flour
2 cups chicken broth
3/4 cup dry sherry
1 tablespoon dried leaf rosemary, crumbled

Preheat oven to 350F (175C). Wash chicken; pat dry with paper towels. Sprinkle chicken with salt, pepper and paprika. In a large skillet, melt 1/2 cup butter. Add chicken pieces, a few at a time, and brown on both sides; remove to 2 large casseroles. When all chicken is browned, melt remaining butter with drippings in skillet. Add mushrooms; sauté until browned. Sprinkle flour over mushrooms. Stir in chicken broth, sherry and rosemary until blended. Cook, stirring constantly, until thickened. Pour mushroom mixture over browned chicken in casseroles. Bake, covered, 1 hour or until chicken is tender. Makes 24 servings.

Meatballs Stroganoff

Oven-browned meatballs save time and dishes.

6 lbs. extra-lean ground beef
2 cups dry breadcrumbs
6 eggs
1 teaspoon dried leaf oregano
1 teaspoon dried leaf marjoram

1 teaspoon dried leaf rosemary
1 tablespoon salt
1/2 teaspoon white pepper
1 pint milk (2 cups)
Stroganoff Sauce, see below

Stroganoff Sauce:
1/2 cup butter
2 large onions, sliced
1/2 cup all-purpose flour
4 cups beef broth

3 pints dairy sour cream (6 cups)
1 tablespoon mild paprika
Salt and pepper to taste

Preheat oven to 400F (205C). In a large bowl, thoroughly combine beef, breadcrumbs, eggs, oregano, marjoram, rosemary, salt, white pepper and milk. Shape into walnut-sized balls. Place meatballs in a single layer on a 15" x 10" jelly-roll pan. Bake 30 minutes or until meatballs are browned; remove to a 6-quart casserole. Prepare Stroganoff Sauce. Pour over meatballs. Reduce oven temperature to 350F (175C). Bake, covered, 30 to 45 minutes or until heated through. Makes 24 servings.

Stroganoff Sauce:
In a large skillet, melt butter. Add onions; sauté 10 minutes or until limp. Stir in flour until blended; cook and stir 2 minutes. Stir in broth; cook, stirring constantly, until thickened. Stir in sour cream, paprika, salt and pepper until blended. Makes about 10 cups.

Spanish Paella

In Spain, many different versions of this classic dish are served.

1 cup olive oil or vegetable oil
5 teaspoons dried leaf oregano
5 teaspoons dried leaf basil
4 garlic cloves, minced
2 teaspoons salt
1 teaspoon black pepper
4 lbs. boneless chicken breasts,
  skinned, cubed
12 chicken legs
20 large shrimp, peeled (leave tails on),
  deveined
2 lbs. chorizo or pepperoni sausages,
  skinned

2 large onions, chopped
1 large green bell pepper, seeded, chopped
2 cups uncooked long-grain white rice
3 cups hot chicken broth
4 large tomatoes, peeled, seeded, chopped
1/8 teaspoon powdered saffron
1 teaspoon chopped fresh cilantro (coriander)
1 (10-oz.) pkg. frozen green peas
12 oz. scallops, cut in quarters
1 (2-oz.) jar sliced pimentos, drained

In a small bowl, combine oil, oregano, basil, garlic, salt and black pepper. Place cubed chicken breasts, chicken legs and shrimp in a large bowl; pour oil mixture over chicken and shrimp. Cover and refrigerate 4 to 24 hours to marinate. In a large skillet, heat 3 tablespoons marinade. Add cubed chicken breasts; sauté 5 minutes or until lightly browned. Remove to a 6-quart casserole or paella pan. In same skillet, brown chicken legs, a few at a time; remove to casserole or pan. Cut chorizo or pepperoni sausages into pieces. Cook in skillet until browned. Remove to casserole or pan with chicken. In skillet, sauté onions and green pepper 15 minutes or until tender. Add rice; stir until browned. Add chicken broth, tomatoes, saffron and cilantro. Add chicken legs to rice mixture in skillet. Bring mixture to a boil; cover and simmer 25 minutes or until chicken and rice are tender and all liquid has been absorbed. Preheat oven to 350F (175C). Add peas and scallops to rice mixture; toss to separate. Turn into casserole or paella pan. Push shrimp into rice mixture. Bake, uncovered, 15 to 20 minutes or until shrimp turn pink. Garnish with pimentos. Makes 12 to 16 servings.

An easy way to remove skin from garlic is to place garlic clove on a cutting board then lay the flat side of a knife on garlic. Pound knife blade with your fist once, partially squashing garlic. Now skin can easily be removed.

Spanish Paella

Seafood & Artichoke Casserole

Crusty French bread and a green salad will round out this elegant casserole.

3 (9-oz.) pkgs. frozen artichoke hearts or
  3 (8-1/2-oz. net dr. wt.) cans
  artichoke hearts
1 (7-oz.) pkg. small macaroni shells
8 oz. fresh, small, whole mushrooms
1/2 cup butter
1/4 cup minced green onion
1/2 cup all-purpose flour
1 qt. whipping cream or half and half,
  heated to boiling (4 cups)
1/2 cup Madeira wine
1 teaspoon salt

1/2 teaspoon white pepper
1/4 teaspoon red (cayenne) pepper
2 (8-oz.) pkgs. fish and crab sticks,
  cut up
2 (6-oz.) pkgs. thawed, frozen,
  snow crabmeat, drained
1 (12-oz.) pkg. thawed, frozen,
  tiny shrimp, drained
1/4 cup lemon juice (1 large lemon)
2 cups shredded Jarlsberg or
  Swiss cheese (8 oz.)
Chopped fresh parsley

Preheat oven to 350F (175C). Butter a 6-quart casserole. Cook frozen artichoke hearts according to package directions; drain and set aside. Rinse, drain and halve canned artichoke hearts; set aside. Cook macaroni according to package directions until tender but firm to the bite; drain. Rinse with cold water to prevent sticking; drain well and set aside. Trim stems from mushrooms; reserve stems for another use. In a large heavy skillet, melt butter. Add mushrooms caps and green onion; sauté 3 minutes or until tender. Stir in flour until blended. Cook, stirring constantly, over low heat 2 minutes; remove from heat. Stir in hot cream or half and half. Return to medium heat and stir until sauce comes to a boil. Reduce heat to low; stir in Madeira. Add salt, white pepper and red pepper. Place fish and crab sticks, crabmeat and shrimp in a large bowl. Pour lemon juice over seafood; toss lightly. Fold in artichoke hearts, cooked macaroni and sauce. Turn seafood mixture into buttered casserole. Sprinkle with cheese. Bake, uncovered, 25 to 30 minutes or until heated through. Garnish with parsley. Makes 16 servings.

Note: If baked in a shallow casserole, baking time will be shorter than given above. If casserole is small in diameter but deep, baking time will be longer because it takes longer for heat to penetrate to center.

 Tip

If you do not have a 6-quart casserole, divide the mixture between 2 (3-quart) casseroles. Reduce the baking time by 5 minutes.

Nacho Casserole

This is layered like lasagna, but with Mexican-style ingredients.

6 lbs. extra-lean ground beef
3 large onions, chopped
3 garlic cloves, minced
3/4 cup chili powder or to taste
4 (15-oz.) cans tomato sauce
2 tablespoons salt
3 cups sliced black olives
3 (4-oz.) cans diced green chilies
Oil for deep-frying
36 (8-inch) corn or flour tortillas

48 oz. small-curd cream-style
    cottage cheese (6 cups)
3 eggs
2 lbs. sliced Monterey Jack cheese
4 cups shredded Cheddar cheese (1 lb.)
1-1/2 cups dairy sour cream
1-1/2 cups chopped green onion
Black olives, avocado wedges and
    tomato wedges

Butter 3 (13" x 9") casseroles. In a large skillet, cook meat in batches until crumbly and no longer pink; remove to a large pot. When all meat is browned, add onions and garlic to skillet; sauté until browned. Add onion mixture to meat along with chili powder, tomato sauce, salt, sliced olives and green chilies. Simmer 15 minutes. Pour oil 2 to 3 inches deep in a wok, deep-fryer or heavy saucepan. Heat oil to 370F (190C) or until a 1-inch cube of bread turns golden brown in 50 seconds. Fry 1 tortilla in hot oil 10 seconds on each side. Drain on paper towels; repeat with remaining tortillas. In a large bowl, combine cottage cheese and eggs. Preheat oven to 350F (175C). Arrange 4 softened tortillas over bottom of each casserole. Spread with 1/3 of meat mixture. Cover with 1/2 of sliced Monterey Jack cheese and 1/2 of cottage-cheese mixture. Top mixture in each casserole with 4 more tortillas. Repeat layering, ending with meat mixture. Top with shredded Cheddar cheese. Bake, uncovered, 30 minutes or until heated through. To serve, top with sour cream and green onion. Garnish with olives, avocado wedges and tomato wedges. Makes 18 to 24 servings.

Dutch Hutspot

This is a complete meat-and-vegetables meal; just add homemade bread!

1 (3-lb.) beef brisket
5 medium onions, chopped
6 medium carrots, chopped
6 medium potatoes, peeled, cubed
1 lb. knockwurst or bratwurst

1/4 cup butter, melted
Salt, black pepper and
    red (cayenne) pepper to taste
Chopped fresh parsley

Preheat oven to 350F (175C). Place beef brisket in a deep 3- or 4-quart casserole. Cover with cold water; bring to a boil. Skim foam from surface of water. Add onions, carrots and potatoes to casserole. Bake, covered, 2 hours or until beef is very tender and vegetables are soft. Using a slotted spoon, remove vegetables; set aside. Add sausages to casserole. Bake, uncovered, 30 minutes longer. In a food processor fitted with a steel blade, process vegetables until smooth. Stir in butter, salt, black pepper and red pepper. Butter a shallow 2-quart casserole. Turn vegetable mixture into buttered casserole. Keep warm. Remove meats from casserole. Peel sausages; cut into 1/2-inch slices. Arrange sausage slices on top of vegetable mixture in casserole. Slice beef brisket across the grain; arrange slices on top of vegetable mixture and sausage slices. Keep warm in a 300F (150C) oven until ready to serve. Garnish with parsley. Makes 10 to 12 servings.

Deep-Dish Ham & Cheese Quiche

For a brunch or luncheon, serve this with a platter of melon.

Press-In Pastry, see below
3 tablespoons butter
1 bunch green onions, chopped,
  including tops
8 oz. fresh mushrooms, sliced

3 cups shredded Swiss cheese (12 oz.)
2 cups diced cooked ham
8 eggs
1 teaspoon dried leaf tarragon
1 pint half and half or whole milk (2 cups)

Press-In Pastry:
2-1/2 cups all-purpose flour
1 cup chilled butter, sliced
1 egg, slightly beaten

1 tablespoon lemon juice
3 tablespoons iced water

Prepare dough for Press-In Pastry. Press into a 14-inch ceramic quiche dish or 13'' x 9'' baking dish, building up dough on sides of dish. Refrigerate 30 minutes. Preheat oven to 400F (205C). Prebake pastry 10 minutes. Increase oven temperature to 425F (220C). In a large skillet, melt butter. Add green onions; sauté 2 minutes. Add mushrooms; sauté 10 minutes or until mushrooms are tender and liquid has evaporated. Sprinkle 1-1/2 cups cheese over bottom of pre-baked pastry shell. Add ham in an even layer, then mushroom mixture and remaining cheese. In a large bowl, beat eggs, tarragon and half and half or milk. Pour over mixture in quiche. Bake 10 minutes; reduce heat to 350F (175C). Bake 30 minutes longer or until set. Serve warm or chilled. Makes 16 servings.

Press-In Pastry:

Place flour and butter in a food processor fitted with a steel blade; process until crumbly. In a small bowl, beat egg, lemon juice and water. Pour into food processor; process until mixture resembles soft crumbs. Pastry can also be made without a food processor: Let butter soften slightly at room temperature, then place in a medium bowl with flour. Using a pastry blender or 2 knives, cut butter into flour until mixture resembles coarse crumbs. Gradually add egg mixture, tossing with a fork until dough resembles soft crumbs. Use as directed above.

Star anise has a mild licorice flavor and is available in Oriental markets and in many whole-food cooperatives. Sesame oil is also available in Oriental markets and many supermarkets.

How to Make Deep-Dish Ham & Cheese Quiche

1/Press dough into a baking dish, building up dough on sides of dish. Refrigerate 30 minutes. Prebake pastry 10 minutes.

2/Layer cheese, ham and mushroom mixture in pastry shell. Pour egg mixture over filling. Bake until set.

Chinese Pot-Roasted Beef

This one-dish meal is even better when made the day before!

1-1/2 tablespoons vegetable oil
1 (3-1/2- to 4-lb.) boneless beef
  chuck roast
2 onions, halved lengthwise,
  sliced lengthwise
1/2 cup soy sauce
1 cup white wine or water
1/4 cup hot ginger brandy or
  1 tablespoon grated fresh gingerroot
4 garlic cloves, bruised, peeled

3 whole star-anise pods
1/2 teaspoon white pepper
1 (16-oz.) can whole tomatoes
4 carrots, cut diagonally in 1-inch pieces
4 celery stalks, cut diagonally in 1-inch
  pieces
2 tablespoons cornstarch
2 tablespoons cold water
1/2 teaspoon sesame oil

In a 6-quart, enamelled, cast-iron casserole, heat oil. Add beef roast. Brown on all sides; remove or push to the side. Add onions; sauté until soft but not browned. Add soy sauce, wine or water, brandy or gingerroot, garlic, anise pods, white pepper and tomatoes with juice. Bake, covered, in a 325F (165C) oven 1-1/2 hours. Add carrots and celery; bake, covered, 1 hour longer or until meat and vegetables are tender. Drain liquid from pot roast into a medium skillet. Bring to a boil; boil until reduced to about 2 cups. In a small bowl, blend cornstarch and water. Whisk into liquid in skillet; cook, stirring constantly, until thickened. Stir in sesame oil; spoon over pot roast and vegetables. Makes 10 to 12 servings.

Whole-Wheat Chicken-Pecan Crepes

You can substitute turkey breast for the chicken in this recipe.

Whole-Wheat Crepes, see below
4 whole chicken breasts, split
1-1/2 cups water
1 cup white wine
1/2 teaspoon salt
1/4 teaspoon white pepper
1/2 cup sliced celery
1 tablespoon chopped fresh parsley

1/2 cup butter
12 oz. fresh mushrooms, sliced
1/2 cup all-purpose flour
1/2 pint whipping cream (1 cup)
1 cup coarsely chopped pecans
1/2 cup shredded Jarlsberg or
   Swiss cheese (2 oz.)

Whole-Wheat Crepes:
2 eggs
1 cup milk
1/2 cup water
1/4 teaspoon salt

1-1/4 cups whole-wheat flour
2 tablespoons butter, melted
Additional water
Butter to cook crepes

Preheat oven to 400F (205C). Lightly butter a shallow 2- to 3-quart casserole or 13'' x 9'' baking dish. Prepare Whole-Wheat Crepes; set aside. In a large saucepan, place chicken breasts, water, wine, salt, white pepper, celery and parsley. Simmer about 30 minutes or until chicken is tender; cool. Strain and measure broth. There should be about 2-1/2 cups; set aside. Remove and discard skin and bones from chicken. Cut chicken into bite-sized pieces. In a large skillet, melt 1/4 cup butter. Add mushrooms; sauté 5 minutes or until lightly browned. Remove mushrooms and set aside. In same skillet, melt remaining butter. Stir in flour until smooth. Whisk in reserved chicken cooking liquid and 1/2 cup cream; bring to a boil, whisking constantly until thickened and smooth. Taste and adjust seasoning, if necessary. Fold mushrooms, chicken and 1/2 cup pecans into sauce. Divide mixture between crepes and roll up. Arrange, seam-side down, in a single layer in buttered casserole. Sprinkle with remaining 1/2 cup pecans. Drizzle with remaining cream. Sprinkle with cheese. Bake, uncovered, 20 minutes or until cheese is melted and edges of crepes are lightly browned. Makes 8 servings.

Whole-Wheat Crepes:
In a medium bowl, whisk eggs, milk, 1/2 cup water and salt. Gradually add flour, whisking constantly until blended. Whisk in melted butter. Strain batter into another medium bowl; cover and refrigerate 1 to 2 hours. To make crepes, whisk batter and add water, 1 tablespoon at a time, to thin batter to consistency of whipping cream. Heat a 6-1/2- to 7-1/2-inch crepe pan or skillet until a drop of water sizzles on it. Lightly butter pan. Ladle about 3 tablespoons batter into pan and swirl to coat surface thinly. Cook 1 to 2 minutes or until edges of crepe begin to brown. Turn and cook about 30 seconds or until other side is spotted brown. Stack crepes as they are cooked. Repeat with remaining batter, adding butter to pan as needed. Makes 16 crepes.

To freeze, place filled crepes in a single layer on a baking sheet; freeze until solid. Immediately remove from baking sheet. Wrap in plastic wrap and foil. Crepes can be prepared a month ahead of serving.

Argentine Puchero

This classic stew requires little tending when baked.

1 cup dried garbanzo beans
1 (1-lb.) ham hock
3 qts. water
2 lbs. beef stew cubes,
2 onions, quartered
1 celery stalk, sliced
2 garlic cloves, minced
3 parsley sprigs
6 black peppercorns
1 bay leaf
2 teaspoons salt
1/2 teaspoon dried leaf oregano
1/2 teaspoon ground cumin

1 lb. chicken wings, disjointed
3 small hot chilies
3 potatoes, peeled, cut in large chunks
3 turnips, quartered
4 carrots, cut in 2-inch chunks
1 small acorn squash, scrubbed, quartered,
   seeded, not peeled
1 small cabbage, cut in eighths
2 fresh or thawed frozen ears of corn,
   cut in 2-inch lengths
8 oz. chorizo sausage
Minced fresh parsley
Hot Sauce, see below

Hot Sauce:
1 to 2 (2-inch) hot peppers, red, yellow or
   green, such as jalapeño or banana
   peppers
1/2 cup lemon juice (2 large lemons)

2 tablespoons minced onion
2 tablespoons minced fresh parsley
1/4 cup peanut oil

Soak garbanzo beans overnight in water to cover; drain. Preheat oven to 325F (165C). In a deep 6-quart casserole, place garbanzo beans, ham hock, 3 quarts water, beef stew cubes, onions, celery, garlic, parsley, peppercorns, bay leaf, salt, oregano and cumin. Bake, covered, 2 hours or until beef is almost tender. Wash chicken wings; pat dry with paper towels. Remove and discard wing-tips or save for broth. Add chicken and all remaining ingredients, except minced parsley and Hot Sauce, to beef mixture. Bake, covered, 1 hour longer or until vegetables are tender. Taste and adjust seasonings. Garnish with minced parsley. Serve with Hot Sauce. Use sauce sparingly until you get accustomed to the hotness! Makes 12 servings.

Hot Sauce:
To handle fresh hot peppers, cover your hands with rubber or plastic gloves. After handling, do not touch your face or eyes. Cut peppers in half lengthwise. Remove and discard seeds and pith. Finely mince flesh. In a small bowl, combine peppers, lemon juice, onion, parsley and oil. Makes about 1 cup.

Rice & Pasta

We generally think of rice and pasta as being fillers or extenders in casseroles. But their roles are not limited to that! Nutritionally, they add complex carbohydrates and plant protein to our diets. They tend to even out the texture of many casseroles, and will absorb liquids which might otherwise be lost. For this reason, precooked rice or pasta that is added to casserole dishes should be slightly undercooked or it will become mushy.

Because rice and pasta are basic ingredients in many countries of the world, classic dishes are international. Casseroles in this chapter reflect a world-wide influence. Many of them are so well known in the area of origin that there are literally thousands of variations of each recipe. When any dish is so indigenous to a country, every cook has his or her own favorite version.

Many of these recipes are handed down from one generation to another. Each generation of cook will automatically update them using ingredients that are available. Some are so updated that the original country may not even recognize them. Something as basic as a lasagna can go a hundred ways. There are two different versions given in this chapter!

A recipe may call for a specific type of rice or pasta. For instance, where you see *long-grain rice,* there is no harm in substituting medium- or short-grain rice. Texture and appearance may be altered, but flavor and nutritional value will be the same. Cooking times are interchangeable between the white and polished rices. However, if you substitute brown rice for white, cooking time is longer. Cooking time for wild rice is about the same as for brown rice. Wild rice can often be used for all or part of the rice in a recipe. Check package directions for recommended cooking times, then make the adjustments in the recipe.

There really are no hard and fast rules about substituting pastas one for another. If a recipe calls for macaroni shells, it is easy to substitute elbow macaroni or any other small macaroni for the shells. Other choices would be rotini spirals, ziti, bows or butterflies, or wheels. It is not easy to substitute spaghetti and noodle types for small pastas. But you can use noodles instead of spaghetti in a dish, knowing that the texture and appearance will be different. You may discover a delicious new combination that will be worth repeating!

Dinner for V.I.P. Guests

Wild-Rice & Mushroom Bake, page 138
Country Captain, page 63, or
Coq au Vin, page 61
Salad of Hearts of Romaine
Herb Vinaigrette
German-Chocolate Soufflé, page 154
Red Wine
Irish Coffee

◆

After-the-Game Buffet

Greek Pastitsio, page 124
Herbed Fresh-Vegetable Bake, page 132
Salad of Shredded Nappa Cabbage
Oil & Vinegar Dressing
Baked Apples with Ginger, page 144
Fruit Juices, Beer
Coffee

◆

Favorite Weekday Dinner for the Family

Old-Fashioned Macaroni & Cheese, page 125
Salad of Sliced Tomatoes & Leaf Lettuce
Italian Dressing
Creamy Baked Custard, page 156

Cuban Beef with Rice & Beans

My casserole version of a classic Cuban dish.

2 cups water
1/2 teaspoon salt
1 cup uncooked long-grain white rice
4 bacon slices
1 large onion, chopped
2 garlic cloves, minced
3 celery stalks, chopped

1 green bell pepper, chopped
1 lb. extra-lean ground beef
1 teaspoon salt
3 tomatoes, peeled, quartered
1 (16-oz.) can kidney beans, drained
1/4 teaspoon black pepper
1/4 teaspoon ground cumin

In a medium saucepan, bring water and 1/2 teaspoon salt to a boil; stir in rice. Bring back to a boil. Cover and reduce heat to low. Cook 20 minutes or until rice is tender and has absorbed all the liquid; set aside. In a large skillet, fry bacon until crisp; drain, crumble and set aside. Add onion, garlic, celery and green pepper to bacon drippings; sauté 10 minutes or until tender. Crumble beef into onion mixture; cook until meat is crumbly and no longer pink. Add 1 teaspoon salt. Turn into a shallow 2-quart casserole or 8-inch-square baking dish. Preheat oven to 375F (190C). In a medium bowl, combine tomatoes, beans, cooked rice, black pepper and cumin. Spread rice mixture in an even layer over meat mixture in casserole. Bake, covered, 25 minutes or until heated through. Garnish with crumbled bacon. Makes 6 servings.

Russian Cabbage Rolls

For an authentic menu, add mashed potatoes and a green salad.

1 large cabbage
1/4 cup butter, melted
1 large onion, chopped
1 lb. extra-lean ground beef
8 oz. lean ground pork
1 cup cooked long-grain white rice

1 teaspoon salt
2 tablespoons minced fresh parsley
1 egg, slightly beaten
2 tablespoons butter, melted
Dilled Sour-Cream Sauce, see below

Dilled Sour-Cream Sauce:
2 tablespoons butter
2 tablespoons all-purpose flour
1 cup tomato juice
1/2 cup water

1/2 pint dairy sour cream (1 cup)
Salt and pepper to taste
1/4 cup chopped fresh dill or
    2 tablespoons dried dill weed

Butter a shallow 3-quart casserole or 13'' x 9'' baking dish. Remove core from cabbage. Place cabbage in a large saucepan of boiling water. Remove leaves as they soften; collect 12 leaves. Remove remaining cabbage and reserve for another use. In a medium skillet, melt 1/4 cup butter. Add onion; sauté until tender but not browned. In a large bowl, combine onion, beef, pork, rice, salt, parsley and egg. Preheat oven to 350F (175C). Divide meat filling between cabbage leaves, placing filling on leaf tip. Roll up, tucking edges around filling. Arrange rolls, seam-side down, in a single layer in buttered casserole. Drizzle with 2 tablespoons melted butter. Bake, uncovered, 45 minutes. Prepare Dilled Sour-Cream Sauce. Remove casserole from oven; pour Dilled Sour-Cream Sauce over cabbage rolls. Bake, uncovered, 15 minutes longer. Makes 6 servings.

Dilled Sour-Cream Sauce:
In a medium saucepan, melt butter. Stir in flour until smooth; cook, stirring constantly, 1 minute. Whisk in tomato juice and water; bring to a boil, whisking constantly until thickened and smooth. Remove from heat; whisk in sour cream, salt, pepper and dill. Makes 2-1/2 cups.

Indian Kedgeree

This classic rice-and-lentil combination makes a good side dish for curry.

1 cup lentils
2 teaspoons salt
1-1/2 cups uncooked long-grain
    converted white rice
2 tablespoons shredded fresh gingerroot
1 (3-inch) cinnamon stick
3 whole cloves

6 black peppercorns
1 bay leaf
6 cardamom pods
5 cups water
1/2 cup butter
2 large onions, sliced
2 hard-cooked eggs, sliced

Parboil lentils in boiling water 10 minutes; drain. Preheat oven to 350F (175C). In a 3-quart casserole, combine lentils, salt, rice, gingerroot, cinnamon, cloves, peppercorns, bay leaf and cardamom. Add 5 cups water. Bake, covered, 1 hour or until rice is tender and liquid is absorbed. In a large skillet, melt butter. Add onions; sauté about 10 minutes or until tender. Top lentil mixture with sautéed onions. Garnish with hard-cooked eggs. Makes 6 to 8 servings.

How to Make Russian Cabbage Rolls

1/Divide meat filling between cabbage leaves, placing filling on leaf tip. Roll up, tucking edges around filling. Arrange, seam-side down, in a single layer in casserole.

2/Bake rolls 45 minutes, then remove from oven. Pour Dilled Sour-Cream Sauce over rolls; bake 15 minutes longer.

Vegetarian Rice Casserole

Grainy and wonderful, this has a chewy texture.

3 cups water
1/2 teaspoon salt
2 cups uncooked long-grain brown rice
2 lbs. fresh spinach
3 tablespoons butter
1 cup chopped onion
2 garlic cloves, minced
4 eggs, beaten
1 cup milk

1-1/2 cups shredded sharp
   Cheddar cheese (6 oz.)
1/4 cup chopped fresh parsley
Salt and black pepper to taste
1/8 teaspoon ground nutmeg
1/8 teaspoon red (cayenne) pepper
1/4 cup sunflower kernels
Paprika

Preheat oven to 350F (175C). Butter a shallow 2-quart casserole or 8-inch-square baking dish. In a medium saucepan, bring water and salt to a boil; stir in rice. Bring back to a boil. Cover and reduce heat to low. Cook 45 minutes or until rice is tender and has absorbed all the liquid. Thoroughly wash spinach; remove and discard stalks and tough ribs. Chop spinach. In a large skillet, melt butter. Add onion and garlic; sauté about 5 minutes or until tender. Add chopped spinach to onion mixture; cook over medium heat 2 minutes. In a large bowl, thoroughly combine cooked rice, onion mixture, eggs, milk, cheese, parsley, salt, black pepper, nutmeg and red pepper. Turn into buttered casserole; sprinkle with sunflower kernels and paprika. Bake, uncovered, 35 minutes or until bubbly and edges are golden. Makes 6 servings.

Sausage & Mushroom Manicotti

Manicotti are large, deliciously stuffed noodles.

14 manicotti shells
Mushroom & Cheese Sauce, see below
1 lb. fresh Italian sausage
1/2 cup sliced green onion
1 garlic clove, minced
8 oz. fresh mushrooms, sliced

1/4 cup all-purpose flour
1-1/2 cups half and half
1/4 teaspoon white pepper
1/4 teaspoon ground nutmeg
1/4 teaspoon rubbed sage
2 tablespoons minced fresh parsley

Mushroom & Cheese Sauce:
2 tablespoons butter
8 oz. fresh mushrooms, sliced
1 (13-oz.) can evaporated milk

2 cups shredded Monterey Jack or
    white Cheddar cheese (8 oz.)
1 tablespoon minced fresh parsley

Preheat oven to 350F (175C). Butter 2 shallow 3-quart casseroles or 2 (13" x 9") baking dishes. Cook manicotti according to package directions until tender but firm to the bite; drain. Rinse with cold water to prevent sticking; drain well and set aside. Prepare Mushroom & Cheese Sauce. In a large skillet, cook sausage until crumbly and no longer pink; drain off fat. Stir in green onion, garlic and mushrooms; sauté 10 minutes or until liquid has evaporated. Stir in flour until blended. Add half and half; cook, stirring constantly, until thickened. Add white pepper, nutmeg and sage. Using a small spoon, stuff each manicotti shell with 1/4 cup sausage mixture. Place in buttered casseroles. Pour Mushroom & Cheese Sauce over filled shells. Bake, uncovered, 15 minutes or until heated through. Garnish with parsley. Makes 7 to 8 servings.

Mushroom & Cheese Sauce:
In a large skillet, melt butter. Add mushrooms; sauté 10 minutes or until liquid has evaporated. Stir in evaporated milk, cheese and parsley. Stir until cheese is melted; set aside. Makes 2-1/2 cups.

Baked Cheddar Noodles with Walnuts

Use purchased or homemade noodles for this meatless main dish.

1 (6-oz.) pkg. egg noodles, cooked, drained
3 tablespoons butter
1 small onion, chopped
2 tablespoons all-purpose flour
1 pint hot milk (2 cups)

1 teaspoon dry mustard
1/2 teaspoon garlic salt
2 cups shredded sharp Cheddar cheese
    (8 oz.)
1/2 cup chopped walnuts

Preheat oven to 375F (190C). Cook noodles according to package directions until tender but firm to the bite; drain. Rinse with cold water to prevent sticking; drain well and set aside. In a medium saucepan, melt butter. Add onion; sauté about 7 minutes or until tender but not browned. Stir in flour until smooth; cook and stir until bubbly. Whisk in hot milk; bring to a boil, whisking constantly until thickened. Whisk in mustard and garlic salt. Arrange 1/2 of noodles in a shallow 2-quart casserole or 8-inch-square baking dish. Top with 1/2 of cheese, then add remaining noodles and cheese. Pour sauce over noodle mixture. Bake, uncovered, 15 minutes or until bubbly. Sprinkle with walnuts; bake, uncovered, 5 minutes longer. Makes 4 servings.

How to Make Sausage & Mushroom Manicotti

1/Using a small spoon, stuff each manicotti shell with 1/4 cup sausage mixture. Place in casseroles.

2/Pour Mushroom & Cheese Sauce over filled shells. Bake until heated through.

Busy-Day Beef Casserole

Assemble this casserole ahead of time, then bake just before dinner.

1 (5-oz.) pkg. medium-width egg noodles	1 (8-oz.) can tomato sauce
1 tablespoon butter	8 oz. cream-style cottage cheese (1 cup)
12 oz. to 1 lb. extra-lean ground beef	1/2 pint dairy sour cream (1 cup)
1 teaspoon salt	6 green onions, chopped, including tops
1/4 teaspoon pepper	3/4 cup sharp Cheddar cheese (3 oz.)
1 teaspoon dried leaf basil	

Cook noodles according to package directions until tender but firm to the bite; drain. Rinse with cold water to prevent sticking; drain well and set aside. In a large skillet, melt butter. Add beef; cook until crumbly and no longer pink. Stir in salt, pepper, basil and tomato sauce. In a large bowl, thoroughly combine cooked noodles, cottage cheese, sour cream and green onions. Preheat oven to 350F (175C). Butter a shallow 2-1/2-quart casserole or 8-inch-square baking dish. Spread 1/2 of noodle mixture over bottom of buttered casserole. Top with 1/2 of beef mixture, then add remaining noodle mixture. Top with remaining beef mixture; sprinkle with Cheddar cheese. Bake, uncovered, 30 minutes or until bubbly and cheese is melted. Makes 6 servings.

Vegetable Lasagna

For a vegetarian meal, this is a satisfying and delicious choice.

9 lasagna noodles
1 lb. fresh spinach
1 tablespoon olive oil or vegetable oil
1/2 cup chopped onion
1 cup shredded carrot
2 cups sliced fresh mushrooms
1 (15-oz.) can tomato sauce
1 (4-1/2-oz.) can chopped black olives
1/2 teaspoon dried leaf basil

1/2 teaspoon dried leaf rosemary
1/4 teaspoon rubbed sage
1/4 teaspoon dried leaf oregano
16 oz. ricotta or cream-style
    cottage cheese (2 cups)
1 lb. Monterey Jack cheese, sliced
1/2 cup grated Parmesan cheese (1-1/2 oz.)
Additional grated Parmesan cheese

Cook lasagna noodles according to package directions; drain. To prevent sticking, lay cooked noodles in a shallow dish with cold water to cover; add 1 teaspoon vegetable oil. Thoroughly wash spinach; remove and discard stalks and tough ribs. Place spinach in a large saucepan with no additional water. Cover and place over high heat; after about 1 minute when steam forms, reduce heat to low and cook 3 minutes. Drain well. Press spinach in a sieve to remove excess liquid. Finely chop spinach; set aside. In a large skillet, heat oil. Add onion, carrot and mushrooms; sauté 10 minutes or until onion is tender and liquid has evaporated. Add tomato sauce, olives and herbs; cook 20 minutes or until vegetables are tender. Preheat oven to 375F (190C). Lightly butter a 13" x 9" baking dish. Drain noodles. Arrange 1/3 of noodles lengthwise in bottom of buttered baking dish. Top with 1/3 of ricotta or cottage cheese, then 1/3 of spinach. Pour over 1/3 of tomato-sauce mixture; sprinkle with 1/3 of Monterey Jack cheese. Repeat layers, placing noodles crosswise in baking dish. Repeat layers for the third time, placing noodles lengthwise. Sprinkle 1/2 cup Parmesan cheese over final layer of Monterey Jack cheese. Bake, uncovered, 40 minutes or until bubbly and top is golden. Let stand 10 minutes before serving. Serve with additional Parmesan cheese. Makes 6 servings.

Italian Sausage & Pasta

This hearty dish is great for a blustery winter day.

1 tablespoon olive oil
2 lbs. fresh Italian sausage,
    casings removed
1 medium onion, chopped
8 oz. fresh mushrooms, quartered
1/2 cup sherry
1/2 cup tomato sauce

1 (10-1/2-oz.) can beef consommé
    plus 1 can water
2 cups uncooked mostaccioli or
    a small pasta such as elbow macaroni
1/2 pint dairy sour cream (1 cup)
Chopped fresh parsley
Grated Parmesan cheese

Preheat oven to 350F (175C). In a large heavy skillet, heat oil. Add sausage; cook until crumbly and no longer pink. Add onion and mushrooms; cook until tender. Turn into a shallow 2-1/2-quart casserole or 8-inch-square baking dish. Pour sherry into skillet and bring to a boil, stirring constantly to scrape up sausage drippings. Pour over sausage mixture in casserole. Stir in tomato sauce, beef consommé, water and pasta. Bake, covered, 1 hour or until pasta is tender. Stir in sour cream. Sprinkle with parsley and Parmesan cheese. Makes 6 servings.

Greek Pastitsio

The aroma of sweet spices makes all the difference in this dish!

1 tablespoon butter or olive oil
1 large onion, finely chopped
1 garlic clove, minced
1 lb. extra-lean ground beef or
    lean ground lamb
2 tablespoons tomato paste
1/2 cup dry red wine
1 teaspoon grated orange peel
1/2 teaspoon ground nutmeg
1/2 teaspoon ground cinnamon
1/2 teaspoon ground allspice
1/2 teaspoon salt

1/4 teaspoon pepper
1 egg, well beaten
1 cup grated kefalotyri, kasseri, or
    Parmesan cheese (3 oz.)
1/4 cup dry breadcrumbs
1 (8-oz.) pkg. elbow macaroni or ziti
2 tablespoons butter
Cream Sauce, see below
1/2 cup dry breadcrumbs
Ground or freshly grated nutmeg
Additional butter

Cream Sauce:
1/4 cup butter
1/4 cup all-purpose flour
1 pint hot milk (2 cups)
Salt and pepper to taste

2 egg yolks
1 cup grated kasseri, Parmesan or
    fontina cheese (3 oz.)

Preheat oven to 350F (175C). Generously butter a 13'' x 9'' baking dish. In a large skillet, melt 1 tablespoon butter or heat oil. Add onion and garlic; sauté about 5 minutes or until tender. Add meat; cook until crumbly and no longer pink. Drain off fat. Stir in tomato paste, wine, orange peel, spices, salt and pepper. Simmer, uncovered, 45 minutes or until liquid has evaporated, stirring occasionally. Remove from heat. Stir in egg, cheese and 1/4 cup breadcrumbs; set aside. Cook macaroni according to package directions until tender but firm to the bite; drain well. Toss hot pasta with 2 tablespoons butter; cover and set aside. Prepare Cream Sauce. Spread 1/2 of macaroni on bottom of buttered baking dish. Cover with meat mixture. Add remaining macaroni in an even layer. Pour Cream Sauce over top and sprinkle with 1/2 cup breadcrumbs and nutmeg; dot with additional butter. Bake, uncovered, 30 minutes or until casserole is set and top is golden brown. Let stand at least 15 minutes before cutting into squares to serve. Makes 6 to 8 servings.

Cream Sauce:
In a large heavy saucepan, melt butter. Stir in flour until smooth. Cook, stirring constantly, over medium heat 2 minutes, being careful not to brown. Whisk in hot milk. Bring to a simmer and cook, stirring constantly, until sauce is the same thickness as whipping cream. Remove from heat; add salt and pepper. In a small bowl, beat egg yolks. Stir some of hot sauce into egg yolks to warm them. Whisk yolk mixture back into sauce; cool. Stir cheese into cooled sauce. Makes about 2 cups.

How to Make Greek Pastitsio

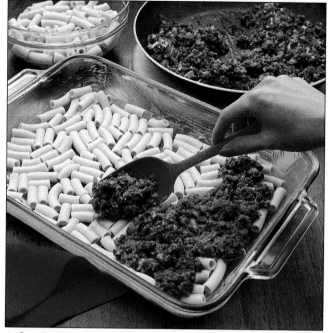

1/Spread 1/2 of macaroni on bottom of baking dish. Cover with meat mixture. Add remaining macaroni in an even layer.

2/Pour sauce over top and sprinkle with breadcrumbs and nutmeg; dot with additional butter. Bake until set and top is golden brown.

Old-Fashioned Macaroni & Cheese

In this family standby, Dijon-style mustard enhances the cheese flavor.

1 (8-oz.) pkg. elbow macaroni
1/4 cup butter
1/4 cup all-purpose flour
1 teaspoon Dijon-style mustard
1/2 teaspoon salt

1/8 teaspoon pepper
1 pint hot milk (2 cups)
2 cups shredded Cheddar cheese (8 oz.)
1 large tomato, sliced

Preheat oven to 375F (190C). Butter a shallow 1-1/2-quart casserole or 8-inch-square baking dish. Cook macaroni according to package directions; drain. Rinse with cold water to prevent sticking; drain well and set aside. In a medium saucepan, melt butter. Stir in flour, mustard, salt and pepper until smooth. Whisk in hot milk; bring to a boil, whisking constantly. Reduce heat to low and simmer 1 minute. Remove from heat; stir in 1-1/2 cups cheese and cooked macaroni. Turn into buttered casserole. Arrange tomato slices over top. Sprinkle remaining cheese over top. Bake, uncovered, 15 minutes or until cheese begins to brown around edges and cheese on tomatoes is melted. Makes 6 servings.

Spinach Lasagna

Spinach gives this favorite dish a special flavor.

1 lb. fresh hot Italian sausage
12 oz. extra-lean ground beef
1 lb. fresh mushrooms, sliced
1 medium onion, chopped
1/2 cup chopped green bell pepper
2 large garlic cloves, minced
1 (28-oz.) can whole tomatoes, drained
1/2 cup sliced black olives

1 small bay leaf
1 (8-oz.) pkg. lasagna noodles
1 (10-oz.) pkg. frozen chopped spinach,
  cooked, drained
16 oz. ricotta cheese (2 cups)
4 cups shredded mozzarella cheese (1 lb.)
1/2 cup grated Parmesan cheese (1-1/2 oz.)
Additional grated Parmesan cheese

In a large heavy saucepan, combine sausage, beef, mushrooms, onion, green pepper and garlic. Cook about 15 minutes or until onion is translucent and meat is crumbly and no longer pink. Drain off liquid. Add tomatoes, tomato paste, olives and bay leaf. Reduce heat to low; cover and simmer 1-1/2 hours, stirring occasionally. Remove and discard bay leaf. Cook lasagna noodles according to package directions; drain. To prevent sticking, lay cooked noodles in a shallow dish with cold water to cover; add 1 teaspoon vegetable oil. Press spinach in a sieve to remove excess liquid. In a medium bowl, combine spinach and ricotta cheese. Preheat oven to 350F (175C). Lightly butter a 13" x 9" baking dish. Spoon a thin layer of sausage mixture over bottom of baking dish. Drain noodles. Arrange 1/2 of noodles over sausage mixture; spread 1/2 of spinach mixture evenly over the top. Sprinkle with 1/2 of mozzarella cheese and 1/4 cup Parmesan cheese. Repeat layers. Bake, uncovered, 40 minutes or until bubbly and top is golden. Let stand 10 minutes before serving. Serve with additional Parmesan cheese. Makes 6 servings.

Broken-Spaghetti Casserole

A great casserole for the family.

6 bacon slices, diced
1 small onion, minced
1 lb. extra-lean ground beef
1-1/2 cups broken uncooked spaghetti
1 (1-lb. 12-oz.) can tomatoes

1 (10-oz.) pkg. frozen green peas
1 (2-oz.) jar diced pimentos, drained
1 (4-1/2-oz.) can sliced black olives
2 cups shredded Cheddar cheese (8 oz.)
Salt and pepper to taste

Preheat oven to 400F (205C). Butter a 3-quart casserole or 13" x 9" baking dish. In a large skillet, cook bacon until crisp; drain off all but 2 tablespoons drippings. Add onion; sauté 3 minutes or until soft but not browned. Add beef; cook until crumbly and no longer pink. Cook spaghetti according to package directions until tender but firm to the bite; drain. Rinse with cold water to prevent sticking; drain well. Add cooked spaghetti, tomatoes with juice, peas, 1/2 of pimentos, 1/2 of olives and 1/2 of cheese to meat mixture; mix with a fork until blended. Add salt and pepper. Turn into buttered casserole; sprinkle with remaining cheese, olives and pimentos. Bake, uncovered, 20 minutes or until cheese is melted. Makes 6 servings.

Vegetables & Side Dishes

Whether you are planning a barbecue, picnic, large or small party, or a roast for dinner, side-dish casseroles are a handy way to round out the menu. The advantages of casseroles apply to the vegetable and side-dish recipes in this chapter: they can be prepared, cooked and served in the same dish. Often they can be assembled as much as a day or two in advance, covered and refrigerated. This is especially handy when you are entertaining and want to keep last-minute preparation to a minimum.

An added advantage is that you will conserve energy when you use the oven for as many dishes as possible at one time. One of the simplest plans is to bake a rice or potato casserole right along with a roast or stew. But there are more innovative creations, too. Vegetables, usually requiring lots of last-minute preparation, can often be assembled a day in advance. Pop them into the oven in time to finish heating for dinner.

Most rules of menu planning indicate that you should not have more than one dish cooked by the same method. Casserole cooking breaks that rule, especially with side dishes. In this menu, three casseroles elegantly complement the main dish and make life easier for the cook!

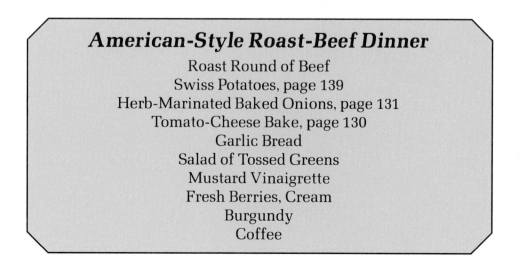

American-Style Roast-Beef Dinner

Roast Round of Beef
Swiss Potatoes, page 139
Herb-Marinated Baked Onions, page 131
Tomato-Cheese Bake, page 130
Garlic Bread
Salad of Tossed Greens
Mustard Vinaigrette
Fresh Berries, Cream
Burgundy
Coffee

Broccoli Baked with Mustard Butter

Bake this casserole along with chicken or a meatloaf.

**2 (10-oz.) pkgs. thawed frozen broccoli,
    drained, or 1-1/2 lbs. fresh broccoli
1/4 teaspoon dried leaf tarragon
1/4 cup water
1/4 cup butter**

**1/4 cup dry white wine
1 teaspoon prepared mustard,
    preferably Dijon-style
1 shallot or 2 green onions, minced
1/4 cup sliced almonds**

Preheat oven to 325F (165C). Butter a shallow 1-quart casserole or 8-inch-square baking dish. If using fresh broccoli, cut off and discard tough ends from stalks. Peel remaining stalks if skin is tough. Cook broccoli in boiling water 5 minutes; drain. Arrange thawed frozen or cooked fresh broccoli in buttered casserole. Sprinkle with tarragon and add water. In a small skillet or saucepan, bring butter, wine, mustard and shallot or green onions to a boil. Cook, stirring constantly, until liquid is reduced to about 2 tablespoons. Drizzle butter mixture over broccoli in casserole. Bake, covered, 30 minutes or until broccoli is tender. Garnish with almonds. Makes 4 to 5 servings.

Broccoli & Tomato Casserole

Assemble this casserole ahead, then bake it at the last minute.

**3 (10-oz.) pkgs. thawed frozen broccoli,
    drained, or 2-1/2 lbs. fresh broccoli
3 large tomatoes, peeled, sliced
1 teaspoon dried leaf basil**

**1/2 pint dairy sour cream (1 cup)
1 cup mayonnaise
2/3 cup grated Parmesan cheese (2 oz.)**

Preheat oven to 325F (165C). Butter a shallow 1-1/2-quart casserole or 8-inch-square baking dish. If using fresh broccoli, cut off and discard tough ends from stalks. Peel remaining stalks if skin is tough. Cook broccoli in boiling water 5 minutes; drain. Arrange thawed frozen or cooked fresh broccoli in buttered casserole. Top with tomato slices and sprinkle with basil. In a small bowl, thoroughly combine sour cream, mayonnaise and Parmesan cheese, reserving a little cheese for topping. Spread cheese mixture over tomato slices; sprinkle with reserved Parmesan cheese. Bake, uncovered, 40 to 45 minutes or until bubbly and lightly browned. Makes 6 to 8 servings.

Burgundy Beef, page 39; Swiss Potatoes, page 139; and Broccoli & Tomato Casserole, above.

Cauliflower, Tomato & Cheese Casserole

Perfect for a buffet table, this is colorful and tastes good!

2 large cauliflowers
1/2 teaspoon salt
Dash of pepper
1/4 teaspoon ground nutmeg

3 cups shredded Cheddar cheese (12 oz.)
1/4 cup butter, melted
3 tomatoes, each cut in 8 wedges
2 tablespoons chopped fresh parsley

Separate cauliflower into flowerets. In a large saucepan, pour water to a depth of 1 inch; add a dash of salt. Bring to a boil; add cauliflowerets. Cook 8 to 15 minutes or until crisp-tender; drain. Preheat oven to 400F (205C). Arrange cooked cauliflowerets in a shallow 3-quart casserole or 13" x 9" baking dish. Sprinkle with 1/2 teaspoon salt, pepper and nutmeg. Cover with 2 cups cheese. Drizzle with melted butter. Tuck in tomato wedges. Sprinkle with remaining 1 cup cheese. Bake, uncovered, 5 minutes or until cheese is melted. Garnish with parsley. Makes 8 servings.

Tomato-Cheese Bake   Photo on page 141.

Whole tomatoes covered with a Swiss-cheese sauce look attractive and appetizing.

1/4 cup butter
1 tablespoon chopped onion
1/4 cup all-purpose flour
1-1/2 cups hot milk
1/2 teaspoon salt
1/8 teaspoon pepper

1/8 teaspoon paprika
2 egg yolks
1/4 cup whipping cream
1/2 cup shredded Swiss cheese (2 oz.)
6 firm tomatoes
1/2 cup grated Parmesan cheese (1-1/2 oz.)

Preheat oven to 425F (220C). Butter a medium, shallow casserole or baking dish. In a large skillet, melt butter. Add onion; sauté 5 minutes or until tender. Stir in flour until blended. Whisk in hot milk; bring to a boil, whisking constantly until thickened and smooth. Stir in salt, pepper and paprika. In a small bowl, combine egg yolks and cream; add small amount of hot sauce. Whisk yolk mixture into remaining sauce in saucepan, stirring until smooth. Cook and stir 1 minute longer without boiling. Stir in Swiss cheese until melted. Cut tops from tomatoes; squeeze out excess seeds and liquid. Arrange in buttered casserole. Pour sauce over tomatoes; sprinkle with Parmesan cheese. Bake, uncovered, 15 to 20 minutes or until bubbly and browned. Makes 6 servings.

Herb-Marinated Baked Onions

Save any leftover marinade to use as a salad dressing.

4 large onions
1 cup vegetable oil
1/2 cup white-wine vinegar
1 teaspoon dried leaf basil
1 teaspoon dried leaf thyme
1 teaspoon dried leaf oregano

1/2 teaspoon sugar
1/2 teaspoon salt
1/4 teaspoon pepper
Paprika
Chopped fresh parsley

Cut onions in 1/2-inch slices. Arrange slices in a single layer in a shallow 3-quart casserole or 13" x 9" baking dish. In a small screwtop jar, combine oil, vinegar, basil, thyme, oregano, sugar, salt and pepper; blend thoroughly. Pour over onions; marinate at room temperature 1 to 2 hours. Preheat oven to 325F (165C). Pour off and reserve marinade from onions. Bake onions, covered, 30 minutes. Uncover, baste with reserved marinade and sprinkle with paprika. Bake, uncovered, 45 minutes to 1 hour longer or until onions are tender. Garnish with parsley. Makes 6 servings.

Ratatouille

Baking is a simple way to cook this classic vegetable combination.

6 tablespoons olive oil or vegetable oil
2 small white onions, sliced
1 garlic clove, minced
1 medium eggplant, cut in 1-inch cubes
2 medium zucchini, cut in 1-inch slices
1 (16-oz.) can tomatoes or 4 fresh
    tomatoes, peeled, quartered

1 teaspoon dried leaf basil
Salt to taste
Quartered fresh tomatoes
Chopped fresh parsley

In a large skillet, heat 3 tablespoons oil. Add onions and garlic; sauté until onions are tender but not browned. In a 3-quart casserole, layer onion mixture, eggplant, zucchini and tomatoes with juice. Sprinkle with basil; pour remaining oil over mixture. Bake, covered, in a 400F (205C) oven 2 hours or until eggplant is very soft; stir twice during cooking. Add salt. If vegetables have too much liquid, pour off some liquid into skillet. Bring to a boil; boil until reduced to a syrupy sauce. Pour over vegetables in casserole. Garnish with quartered tomatoes and parsley. Serve hot or at room temperature. Makes 6 servings.

Clapshot

This is a Scottish dish from the Orkney Islands.

4 medium potatoes, peeled, cubed (1 lb.)
5 to 6 medium turnips, peeled, cubed (1 lb.)
1 tablespoon chopped chives
1/2 to 1 teaspoon salt

1/4 teaspoon white pepper
1/4 cup butter, melted
1 tablespoon chopped chives

Place potatoes and turnips in a large saucepan with water to cover. Bring to a boil; simmer about 20 minutes or until vegetables are tender. Drain. Preheat oven to 450F (230C). With an electric mixer, beat turnips and potatoes together until mashed and very smooth. Beat in 1 tablespoon chopped chives, salt, white pepper and 1/2 of butter. Turn into a shallow 1-quart casserole. Smooth top, then with the edge of a spoon, make indentations in top to form a pattern. Drizzle with remaining butter. Bake, uncovered, 15 minutes or until top is browned. Garnish with 1 tablespoon chopped chives. Makes 4 servings.

Herbed Fresh-Vegetable Bake

Substitute other vegetables in season in this colorful casserole.

6 medium carrots
3 medium zucchini, cut diagonally
   in 1/4-inch slices
1 cup cherry tomatoes
1 cup herb-seasoned croutons
2 tablespoons cornstarch

1-1/2 cups milk
1/4 cup butter
1 teaspoon dried leaf basil
1 teaspoon salt
1/4 teaspoon pepper

Preheat oven to 375F (190C). Butter a shallow 1-1/2- to 2-quart casserole or 8-inch-square baking dish. Cut carrots into julienne strips by cutting first into 2-inch lengths, then slice lengthwise. Stack slices and cut into 1/4-inch strips. Drop carrots into boiling salted water; cook 10 minutes or until crisp-tender. Drain well. Place carrots, zucchini and cherry tomatoes in buttered casserole. Sprinkle with croutons. In a small saucepan, blend cornstarch and milk; bring to a boil. Cook, stirring constantly, until thickened and smooth. Whisk in butter until melted. Add basil, salt and pepper. Pour over vegetables in casserole. Bake, covered, 20 to 30 minutes or until bubbly and heated through. Makes 6 servings.

How to Make Clapshot

1/Turn potato mixture into a shallow 1-quart casserole. Smooth top, then with the edge of a spoon, make indentations in top to form a pattern.

2/Drizzle melted butter over potato mixture. Bake until browned. Garnish with chopped chives.

Zucchini & Green-Pepper Casserole

This is a great buffet dish for entertaining.

8 cups diced fresh zucchini
1 large green bell pepper, chopped
1 large onion, minced
1 cup dry breadcrumbs
1 cup shredded sharp Cheddar cheese
  (4 oz.)

1/2 cup olive oil
1 teaspoon dried leaf basil
1/2 teaspoon salt
1/4 teaspoon black pepper
2 eggs, beaten

Preheat oven to 350F (175C). Butter a shallow 3-quart casserole or 13" x 9" baking dish. In a large bowl, combine all ingredients. Turn into buttered casserole. Bake, uncovered, 45 minutes or until vegetables are tender and top is lightly browned. Makes 6 to 8 servings.

Baked Chilies Rellenos

This is great as a lunch, brunch or side dish.

8 oz. Monterey Jack Cheese
2 (4-oz.) cans whole peeled green chilies
6 eggs, separated

1/3 cup all-purpose flour
3/4 teaspoon salt

Preheat oven to 400F (205C). Butter a shallow 2-quart casserole or 8-inch-square baking dish. Cut cheese into strips 1/2 inch thick and 3 inches long. Remove and discard seeds from chilies. Cut each chili lengthwise into 3 strips. Wrap a chili strip around each piece of cheese; set aside. In a large bowl, beat egg whites until soft peaks form; set aside. Without washing beaters, in a small bowl, beat egg yolks until creamy; beat in flour and salt. Fold egg whites into yolk mixture. Spread 1/2 of egg mixture in bottom of buttered casserole. Top with chili-wrapped cheese. Add remaining egg mixture. Bake, uncovered, 15 to 20 minutes or until set. Makes 6 servings.

Vegetables Mexicali

This is hearty enough to be a vegetarian main dish.

2 tablespoons vegetable oil
3 to 4 medium zucchini, sliced (about 1 lb.)
1 medium, white onion, chopped
1 small green bell pepper, chopped
4 eggs, slightly beaten
2 (4-oz.) cans diced green chilies
Salt, black pepper and ground cumin
  to taste

6 (6-inch) corn tortillas
2 tablespoons all-purpose flour
1/2 pint dairy sour cream (1 cup)
3 cups shredded Monterey Jack or
  Cheddar cheese (12 oz.)

Preheat oven to 350F (175C). In a large skillet, heat oil. Add zucchini, onion and green pepper; sauté about 5 minutes or until crisp-tender. Add eggs and stir until barely set. Remove skillet from heat; stir in chilies, salt, black pepper and cumin. Cut each tortilla into 6 wedges. In a small bowl, blend flour and sour cream. Arrange 1/2 of tortilla wedges in a shallow 2-quart casserole or 8-inch-square baking dish. Add 1/2 of vegetable mixture, then 1/2 of sour-cream mixture. Top with 1/2 of cheese. Repeat layers ending with cheese. Bake, uncovered, 30 minutes or until or bubbly. Makes 6 servings.

How to Make Baked Chilies Rellenos

1/Cut cheese into strips 1/2 inch thick and 3 inches long. Cut each chili lengthwise into 3 strips. Wrap a chili strip around each piece of cheese.

2/ Spread 1/2 of egg mixture in bottom of casserole. Top with chili-wrapped cheese. Add remaining egg mixture. Bake until set.

Hominy & Chili Casserole

This is delicious served with roast pork or ham.

2 (20-oz.) cans whole white hominy
2 tablespoons grated onion
1/2 pint whipping cream (1 cup)
1 tablespoon cornstarch
1/2 teaspoon salt

1 cup shredded Monterey Jack cheese (4 oz.)
1 (4-oz.) can diced green chilies
1/4 cup dry breadcrumbs
2 tablespoons butter

Preheat oven to 350F (175C). Drain hominy and turn into a 2-quart casserole or 8-inch-square baking dish. Stir in onion. In a small bowl, blend cream, cornstarch and salt; pour over hominy. Stir in cheese and green chilies. Top with breadcrumbs and dot with butter. Bake, uncovered, 30 minutes or until bubbly and heated through. Set under broiler briefly to brown top, if necessary. Makes 6 to 8 servings.

Potato, Turnip & Leek Chartreuse

This is simply mashed potatoes and turnips layered with cabbage!

1 medium cabbage, cored
5 tablespoons butter
1 cup diced boiled ham
2 large garlic cloves
1/4 cup beef broth
1-1/2 lbs. potatoes, peeled, cooked, mashed
1-1/2 lbs. turnips or rutabagas,
   peeled, cooked, pureed

1 large leek, white part only,
   sliced (2 cups)
1/3 cup whipping cream
2 egg yolks
1/4 teaspoon ground nutmeg
Salt and pepper to taste

Bring a large pot of water to a boil. Add cabbage; boil about 5 minutes or until leaves can be separated from head. Return 1/2 of leaves to water; cook 10 minutes in boiling water. Using tongs, transfer cabbage leaves to a colander. Repeat with remaining leaves. In a large skillet, melt 1/2 of butter. Add ham and garlic; sauté 3 minutes. In a medium bowl, combine ham, garlic, broth, potatoes and turnips or rutabagas. In a large heavy skillet, melt remaining butter. Add leek; cover and cook about 20 minutes or until tender, stirring occasionally. Stir into potato mixture. Stir in cream, egg yolks, nutmeg, salt and pepper. Preheat oven to 400F (205C). Butter a 3-quart soufflé dish. Cut out remaining tough stems from cabbage leaves. Pat leaves dry with paper towels. Sprinkle with salt and pepper. Use 3/4 of cabbage leaves to line buttered dish, letting part of leaves hang over side of dish. Place 1/2 of potato mixture in lined dish. Top with 1/2 of remaining cabbage leaves. Top with remaining potato mixture, then cover with remaining cabbage leaves. Fold overhanging leaves over filling. Cover with buttered parchment or waxed paper, then foil. Bake 20 minutes. Reduce temperature to 350F (175C). Bake 1-1/2 hours longer or until heated through. Let stand 5 minutes. To loosen, run a knife around edge of dish; turn out onto a warm platter. Cut into wedges to serve. Makes 6 servings.

Kentucky Bourbon Sweet Potatoes

Try this for your next holiday dinner!

3 (23-oz.) cans sweet potatoes
1/2 cup packed brown sugar
1/3 cup bourbon

1/2 cup butter, room temperature
1/2 teaspoon vanilla extract
2 cups chopped pecans

Preheat oven to 350F (175C). Butter a shallow 2-quart casserole or 8-inch-square baking dish. In a food processor fitted with a steel blade, process sweet potatoes until mashed. Add sugar, bourbon, butter and vanilla; process until smooth and well-blended. Or, warm potatoes in a medium saucepan. Place warmed potatoes in a large bowl; mash with an electric mixer. Beat in sugar, bourbon, butter and vanilla. Turn into buttered casserole. Sprinkle with pecans. Bake, uncovered, 30 minutes or until heated through. Makes 6 to 8 servings.

How to Make Potato, Turnip & Leek Chartreuse

1/Use 3/4 of cabbage leaves to line dish, letting part of leaves hang over side of dish. Layer potato mixture and remaining cabbage leaves in dish. Cover and bake.

2/Let baked dish stand 5 minutes. To loosen, run a knife around edge of dish; turn out onto a warm platter. Cut into wedges to serve.

Old-Fashioned Corn Soufflé

Serve this as a main dish for lunch with a green salad.

1 tablespoon butter
1/4 cup grated Parmesan cheese (3/4 oz.)
1/4 cup butter
1/4 cup all-purpose flour
1/4 teaspoon salt
Dash of pepper
1 cup milk

1 cup shredded Cheddar cheese (4 oz.)
4 eggs, separated
1 (10-oz.) pkg. frozen whole-kernel corn, cooked, drained
6 bacon slices, crisp-cooked, crumbled
1/4 teaspoon cream of tartar

Preheat oven to 350F (175C). Using 1 tablespoon butter, butter a 1-1/2-quart soufflé dish. Sprinkle with Parmesan cheese and rotate dish to coat bottom and sides evenly. In a medium saucepan, melt 1/4 cup butter. Stir in flour, salt and pepper until smooth. Remove from heat; gradually stir in milk. Bring to a boil, stirring constantly. Boil and stir 1 minute. Remove from heat; stir in Cheddar cheese. In a small bowl, blend small amount of hot cheese mixture into egg yolks; return to saucepan and blend thoroughly. Stir in corn and bacon; set aside. In a large bowl, beat egg whites until frothy. Add cream of tartar; beat until soft peaks form. Fold cheese mixture into egg whites. Turn into prepared soufflé dish. Bake, uncovered, 45 to 50 minutes or until puffy and lightly browned. Serve immediately. Makes 6 servings.

Curried Rice & Carrots   **Photo on page 55.**

This goes well with baked, broiled or barbecued chicken.

3/4 cup uncooked long-grain white rice
3 large carrots, thinly sliced
1 teaspoon curry powder

1 green onion, sliced
1/4 cup raisins
1-1/2 cups boiling chicken broth

Place rice in a shallow baking dish. Place in oven. Set oven to preheat to 400F (205C). Remove rice after 8 to 10 minutes or when lightly browned. Butter a 1-1/2-quart casserole. In buttered casserole, combine carrots, curry powder, green onion, raisins and toasted rice. Stir in boiling broth. Bake, uncovered, 25 minutes or until rice is tender and has absorbed all the liquid. Before serving, fluff with a fork. Makes 4 to 6 servings.

Easy Rice & Tomato Pilaf

Bake this pilaf along with a roast or chicken.

3 tablespoons butter
1 cup uncooked long-grain white rice
2 tomatoes, peeled, chopped
2 cups water

1/2 teaspoon salt
1 tablespoon minced fresh basil or
    2 teaspoons dried leaf basil

Preheat oven to 325F (165C). Combine all ingredients in a 1-1/2-quart casserole. Bake, covered, 1 hour or until rice is tender and has absorbed all the liquid. Before serving, fluff with a fork. Makes 6 servings.

Wild-Rice & Mushroom Bake

This is the most foolproof way to cook wild rice!

1 cup uncooked wild rice
2-1/2 cups beef or chicken broth
1/2 teaspoon dried leaf thyme
1/2 teaspoon dried leaf marjoram
1/8 teaspoon pepper

Salt to taste
2 tablespoons butter
1 medium onion, coarsely chopped
2 small carrots, cut in 1/4-inch dice
8 oz. fresh mushrooms, sliced

Preheat oven to 325F (165C). Butter a 2-quart casserole. Rinse wild rice in 3 changes of hot tap water or until water is no longer cloudy. Place in buttered casserole. Add broth, thyme, marjoram, pepper and salt. Amount of salt depends on salt in broth. Start with 1 teaspoon if broth is unsalted. In a large skillet, melt butter. Add onion, carrots and mushrooms; sauté about 10 minutes or until onion is tender and liquid has evaporated. Stir onion mixture into rice mixture in casserole. Bake, covered, 1 hour or until rice is tender and has absorbed all the liquid. Before serving, fluff with a fork. Makes 6 servings.

Swiss Potatoes   Photo on page 129.

Long, slow baking produces a slightly crunchy crust.

4 large baking potatoes,
   peeled (about 2 lbs.)
1/4 cup butter, room temperature
3 garlic cloves, minced
2-1/2 cups shredded Swiss cheese (10 oz.)

1 small onion, chopped
Salt, pepper and ground nutmeg to taste
2 eggs
1 pint whipping cream (2 cups)

Preheat oven to 325F (165C). Thinly slice potatoes; to prevent browning, place in a bowl of iced water until ready to use. Combine 2 tablespoons butter with 1/3 of minced garlic; rub mixture on bottom and sides of a shallow 2-quart casserole or gratin dish. Drain potatoes; pat dry with paper towels. Arrange 1/4 of potato slices in an overlapping layer in buttered casserole. In a medium bowl, toss 2 cups cheese with onion and remaining minced garlic. Spoon 1/4 of cheese mixture over potatoes in casserole, then sprinkle with salt, pepper and nutmeg. Repeat layering with potatoes, cheese mixture and seasonings 3 more times. In a medium bowl, beat eggs and cream; spoon over potato mixture. Sprinkle with remaining 1/2 cup cheese and dot with remaining butter. Bake, uncovered, 1-1/2 hours or until top is browned and potatoes are very tender. Makes 6 servings.

French Potato Gratin

This is known as Gratin Dauphinois, *a favorite in French restaurants.*

3 large baking potatoes,
   peeled (1-1/2 lbs.)
1 garlic clove
Pinch of salt
1 tablespoon butter
1 teaspoon salt

1/2 teaspoon pepper
1/8 teaspoon ground nutmeg
1/3 cup shredded aged Swiss or
   Jarlsberg cheese (1-1/2 oz.)
1-1/2 cups half and half or
   whipping cream

Slice potatoes very thinly; to prevent browning, place in a bowl of iced water until ready to use. Crush garlic with pinch of salt; work mixture into butter. Spread over bottom and sides of a shallow 1-1/2-quart casserole or gratin dish. Preheat oven to 350F (175C). Drain potatoes; pat dry with paper towels. Arrange slices neatly in overlapping rows in buttered casserole. Sprinkle with 1 teaspoon salt, pepper, nutmeg and 1/2 of cheese. In a small saucepan, bring half and half or cream to a boil. Pour over potato mixture in casserole. Sprinkle with remaining cheese. Bake, uncovered, 45 minutes to 1 hour or until potatoes are browned and very tender. Makes about 6 servings.

Tip
_____

If you have a food processor with several slicing blades, use the 2-mm. blade to slice the potatoes.

Hot Baked Potato Salad

Great with barbecued sausages, chicken or hamburgers!

8 small red-skinned potatoes (2 lbs.)	**1/3 cup white-wine vinegar**
6 bacon slices	**2 tablespoons Dijon-style mustard**
3/4 cup chopped green onion, including tops	**1 tablespoon sugar**
3/4 cup chopped green bell pepper	**1 teaspoon celery seeds**
3/4 cup chopped celery	**1 teaspoon salt**
1/2 pint dairy sour cream (1 cup)	**2 hard-cooked eggs, sliced**
1/3 cup mayonnaise	**Chopped fresh parsley**

Scrub potatoes; it is not necessary to peel them. Cut into 1/2- to 1-inch chunks; place on a rack in a steamer. Cook, covered, over boiling water 10 to 15 minutes or until tender; cool. In a medium skillet, cook bacon until crisp. Drain, reserving 2 tablespoons drippings. Crumble bacon. In a shallow 2-quart casserole, combine bacon, potatoes, green onion, green pepper and celery. Preheat oven to 400F (205C). In a small bowl, blend reserved bacon drippings, sour cream, mayonnaise, vinegar, mustard, sugar, celery seeds and salt. Pour evenly over potato mixture; stir gently to mix well. Bake, uncovered, about 20 minutes or until bubbly. Garnish with hard-cooked eggs and parsley. Makes 6 servings.

Bulgur Baked with Raisins & Pine Nuts

Serve this with roast duck, turkey or curry dishes.

1 cup bulgur or cracked wheat	**1/2 cup golden raisins**
2 cups boiling water	**1/2 cup dark raisins**
1 teaspoon salt	**1/2 cup toasted pine nuts or**
1 teaspoon dried leaf basil	**slivered almonds**

Preheat oven to 300F (150C). Butter a 1-quart casserole. Combine bulgur or cracked wheat, water, salt, basil and raisins in buttered casserole. Bake, covered, 30 to 45 minutes or until bulgur or cracked wheat is tender and has absorbed all the liquid. Before serving, fluff with a fork and garnish with toasted nuts. Makes 6 servings.

Bulgur is a very nutritious food. It is made from wheat that is cooked, dried and then cracked.

Tomato-Cheese Bake, page 130, and Hot Baked Potato Salad, above.

Cabbage & Mushrooms au Gratin

Cabbage baked with cream becomes sweet flavored.

1 small cabbage, cored
1-1/2 cups whipping cream
1/4 cup ground nutmeg
2 tablespoons butter

8 oz. fresh mushrooms, thinly sliced
Salt and pepper to taste
2 tablespoons grated Parmesan cheese

Butter a shallow 5-cup casserole or gratin dish. Cut cabbage into 2- to 3-inch chunks. By hand or in a food processor fitted with a steel blade, finely chop cabbage. In a large saucepan, bring about 2 quarts water to a boil. Add cabbage; bring to a boil and boil 3 minutes. Drain and rinse under cold water; squeeze out excess liquid. In a large heavy saucepan, combine cooked cabbage and 1 cup cream. Simmer, uncovered, 25 minutes or until cream is absorbed and cabbage is dry, stirring frequently. Add nutmeg. Preheat oven to 375F (190C). In a large skillet, melt butter. Add mushrooms; sauté 10 minutes or until liquid has evaporated. Add remaining 1/2 cup cream to mushrooms. Simmer, stirring constantly, 3 minutes or until cream is absorbed and mushrooms are dry; add salt and pepper. Spoon mushroom mixture into buttered casserole; spoon cabbage mixture over top. Sprinkle with Parmesan cheese. Bake, uncovered, 5 minutes or until heated through. Preheat broiler; broil about 5 inches from heat until cheese is golden. Makes 6 servings.

Mushrooms au Gratin

Serve this as a hot first course or as a main course for lunch.

3 tablespoons butter
2 tablespoons minced shallots or green onion
1-1/4 lbs. fresh mushrooms, sliced
1 teaspoon salt
1 teaspoon lemon juice
2 tablespoons sherry

1-1/2 cups whipping cream
3 eggs
Pinch of ground nutmeg
1/8 teaspoon pepper
1/4 cup shredded Swiss cheese (1 oz.)

Preheat oven to 375F (190C). Butter a 1-1/2-quart gratin dish or 6 to 8 individual gratin dishes. In a large heavy skillet, melt butter. Add shallots or green onion; sauté 2 minutes. Stir in mushrooms, salt, lemon juice and sherry. Cook 10 minutes or until liquid has evaporated. Add 1 cup cream. Bring to a boil; boil about 5 minutes or until cream is reduced to a thick sauce. In a medium bowl, beat eggs and remaining 1/2 cup cream. Stir mushroom mixture into egg mixture; turn into buttered dish or individual dishes. Sprinkle with nutmeg, pepper and cheese. Bake, uncovered, 15 to 20 minutes or until bubbly. Makes 6 to 8 servings.

Desserts

Casserole desserts have a homey, warm, down-on-the-farm connotation. Think of orchard-fresh apples bubbling in a deep pot, or freshly picked blueberries nestling under a crisp buttery topping. Lemony puddings, creamy baked custards and melt-in-the-mouth apple desserts are reminiscent of supper at Grandmother's house! Oven-simmered rice pudding from Scandinavia makes the perfect dessert for a hearty holiday meal. Top with cinnamon sugar or stewed fruit which has baked in the oven, along with the turkey or spicy ham.

Desserts from casseroles have the same convenience as other main- or side-dish casseroles. They can be made ahead, they hold well, and they are often delicious served hot, at room temperature, or even chilled.

If you serve the dessert buffet-style or pass it at the table, it is always more appealing when you select your prettiest appropriate casserole. For instance, I hesitate to bake the German-Chocolate Soufflé in my soufflé dish decorated with garlic and parsley motifs!

For a change, consider baking these desserts in individual casseroles, attractive custard cups or ramekins. Adjust the baking time accordingly; usually individual desserts will bake in about one-third less time than full-size casseroles.

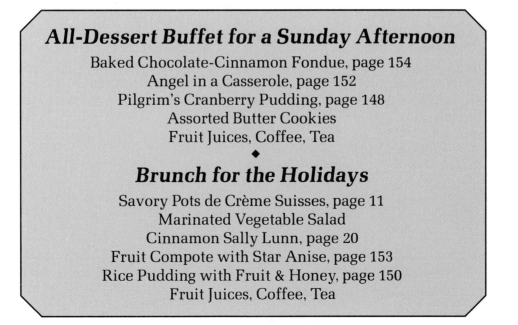

All-Dessert Buffet for a Sunday Afternoon

Baked Chocolate-Cinnamon Fondue, page 154
Angel in a Casserole, page 152
Pilgrim's Cranberry Pudding, page 148
Assorted Butter Cookies
Fruit Juices, Coffee, Tea

♦

Brunch for the Holidays

Savory Pots de Crème Suisses, page 11
Marinated Vegetable Salad
Cinnamon Sally Lunn, page 20
Fruit Compote with Star Anise, page 153
Rice Pudding with Fruit & Honey, page 150
Fruit Juices, Coffee, Tea

Apple-Custard Brûlée

Crème Brûlée is a classic custard dessert—this one adds apples!

4 medium cooking apples	3 eggs
2 tablespoons butter	1 teaspoon vanilla extract
1/2 teaspoon ground cardamom	1 pint half and half or whole milk (2 cups)
1/3 cup granulated sugar	1/2 cup packed brown sugar

Preheat oven to 325F (165C). Peel, core and thinly slice apples. In a large ovenproof skillet, melt butter. Add apples, cardamom and granulated sugar; sauté 5 minutes or until apples are golden and liquid is syrupy. In a medium bowl, beat eggs, vanilla and half and half or milk. Pour over apples in skillet. Bake, uncovered, 30 to 45 minutes or until custard is set. Cool and refrigerate. Before serving, preheat broiler. Press brown sugar through a sieve in an even layer over top of custard. Broil about 6 inches from heat until brown sugar is melted. Serve immediately. Makes 6 servings.

Baked Apples with Ginger   *Photo on page 149.*

Delicious served warm with thick chilled cream to pour over!

4 to 6 large baking apples	1 cup sugar
1 cup chopped candied ginger	1 (6-oz.) jar red-currant or
1 cup chopped filberts or almonds	crab-apple jelly
1 cup hot water	Additional sugar

Preheat oven to 350F (175C). Butter a shallow 2-1/2- to 3-quart casserole. Core apples almost to the bottom; peel halfway down. In a medium bowl, mix ginger and nuts. Fill apple cavities with nut mixture. Place filled apples in buttered casserole. Place remaining nut mixture around apples. In a medium bowl, combine hot water, 1 cup sugar and jelly. Pour into casserole. Bake, uncovered, 45 minutes or until apples are tender, basting 3 or 4 times during cooking. Preheat broiler. Sprinkle apples with additional sugar. Broil 4 inches from heat 1 minute or until browned. Makes 4 to 6 servings.

To prevent peeled sliced apples from turning brown, place apple slices in a mixture of 2 tablespoons lemon juice and 1 cup water until ready to use.

How to Make Apple-Custard Brûlée

1/Press brown sugar through a sieve in an even layer over top of custard.

2/Broil about 6 inches from heat until brown sugar is melted. Serve immediately.

Apple Streusel

This is a deep-dish apple pie without the crust.

2/3 cup all-purpose flour	About 3/4 cup granulated sugar
1/3 cup packed brown sugar	2 tablespoons all-purpose flour
1/3 cup butter	1 teaspoon ground cinnamon
3 lbs. cooking apples	1/2 teaspoon ground nutmeg
(about 8 cups sliced)	Lightly whipped cream

Preheat oven to 350F (175C). Butter a 1-1/2-quart casserole. To make topping, in a large bowl, mix 2/3 cup flour and brown sugar. With a pastry blender or 2 knives, cut in butter until mixture resembles coarse crumbs; set aside. Peel, core and thinly slice apples. As they are sliced, place slices in a bowl of cold water and lemon juice to prevent darkening. When all apples are sliced, drain and pat dry with paper towels; place in a large bowl. If apples are very tart, use full amount of granulated sugar; if less tart, adjust sugar to taste. In a small bowl, mix granulated sugar, 2 tablespoons flour, cinnamon and nutmeg. Toss this mixture lightly with apples. Turn into buttered casserole. Sprinkle topping over apples, patting it down evenly. Bake, uncovered, 45 minutes to 1 hour or until apples are tender and juices bubble around edge. Serve warm or at room temperature with lightly whipped cream. Makes 8 servings.

Apple-Cheese Cobbler

A hearty dessert for a cold evening.

Cobbler Topping, see below
1-1/2 lbs. cooking apples,
    sliced (about 4 cups)
1/3 cup sugar
2 tablespoons quick-cooking tapioca
1/2 teaspoon ground cinnamon

1/4 teaspoon ground nutmeg
1-1/4 cups water
2 tablespoons butter
1 cup shredded sharp Cheddar cheese (4 oz.)
Vanilla Sauce, see below

Cobbler Topping:
1 cup all-purpose flour
2 tablespoons sugar
1-1/2 teaspoons baking powder
1/4 teaspoon salt

1/3 cup butter
1 egg
1/4 cup milk

Vanilla Sauce:
1 pint milk (2 cups)
1 tablespoon cornstarch
1/4 cup sugar

2 teaspoons vanilla extract
1 teaspoon butter

Preheat oven to 425F (220C). Butter an 8- or 9-inch-square baking dish. Prepare Cobbler Topping; set aside. Peel, core and thinly slice apples. As they are sliced, place slices in a bowl of cold water and lemon juice to prevent darkening. When all apples are sliced, drain and pat dry with paper towels. Place in a medium bowl. Add sugar; mix well and set aside. In a medium saucepan, combine tapioca, cinnamon, nutmeg, water and butter; let stand 5 minutes. Bring to a boil over medium heat and boil 7 to 8 minutes or until thickened. Add apple mixture and bring to a boil again, stirring constantly. Cook, stirring constantly, 5 minutes. Turn into buttered baking dish. Sprinkle with cheese. Drop rounded spoonfuls of Cobbler Topping onto cheese layer. Bake, uncovered, 20 to 25 minutes or until cobbler is lightly browned. Prepare Vanilla Sauce. Serve cobbler warm with Vanilla Sauce. Makes 6 servings.

Cobbler Topping:
In a medium bowl, mix flour, sugar, baking powder and salt. With a pastry blender or 2 knives, cut in butter until mixture resembles coarse crumbs. In a small bowl, beat egg and milk; stir into flour mixture until a soft dough forms.

Vanilla Sauce:
In a medium saucepan, blend milk, cornstarch and sugar. Bring to a boil over medium-low heat, stirring constantly; cook and stir until slightly thickened. Stir in vanilla and butter. Makes about 2 cups.

Old-Americana Fruit Clafouti

Clafouti batter is light and pancake-like so it's not a cobbler!

2 tablespoons butter
1/4 cup all-purpose flour
1/3 teaspoon salt
2 eggs
2 tablespoons dairy sour cream
1/3 cup milk
1 tablespoon grated lemon peel
1/4 cup sugar

2-1/2 to 3 cups sliced pears, sliced
    apples, sliced bananas, sliced peaches
    halved apricots, strawberries,
    blueberries, raspberries, pitted
    cherries or halved pitted plums
2 tablespoons dark rum or
    fruit-flavored liqueur
Whipping cream

Place butter in a 1-quart soufflé dish. Set in oven as it preheats to 375F (190C). When butter is melted, spread evenly over dish. In a large bowl, beat flour, salt, eggs, sour cream, milk and lemon peel. In a large bowl, combine sugar, prepared fruit and rum or liqueur. Pour batter into buttered dish. Top with fruit mixture. Bake, uncovered, 35 to 40 minutes or until batter is puffed and top is lightly browned. Serve hot with cream. Makes 6 servings.

Pumpkin-Almond Pudding *Photo on page 149.*

Try this instead of pie for your next holiday dinner.

1 (16-oz.) can pumpkin
2 eggs, slightly beaten
1 cup packed brown sugar
3/4 cup toasted slivered almonds
2 tablespoons raisins
2 tablespoons butter

2 tablespoons all-purpose flour
1-1/2 cups milk
1-1/2 teaspoons pumpkin-pie spice
1/4 teaspoon salt
1/4 teaspoon vanilla extract

Preheat oven to 350F (175C). Butter a 1-1/2-quart soufflé dish or deep 1-1/2-quart casserole. In a large bowl, thoroughly combine pumpkin, eggs, 1/2 cup sugar, 1/4 cup almonds and 1 tablespoon raisins; set aside. In a medium, heavy saucepan, melt butter. Stir in flour until browned. Whisk in milk; cook, whisking constantly, over low heat until thickened and smooth. In a small bowl, mix pie spice, salt and remaining sugar. Stir into sauce; add vanilla. Blend 1/2 of sauce with pumpkin mixture; pour into buttered dish. Pour remaining sauce over top; sprinkle with remaining almonds and raisins. Bake, uncovered, 40 minutes or until set. Serve warm or chilled. Makes 8 servings.

Pilgrim's Cranberry Pudding

This easy pudding is one to remember during the holidays!

1 egg
1/2 cup light molasses
1/3 cup warm water
1-1/3 cups all-purpose flour
1 teaspoon baking powder

1/2 teaspoon baking soda
2 cups fresh or frozen cranberries
Frosted Cranberries, see below
Caramel Sauce, see below

Frosted Cranberries:
1 egg white
1-1/2 cups fresh or thawed
   frozen cranberries

1/3 cup sugar

Caramel Sauce:
2 tablespoons butter
1/2 pint whipping cream (1 cup)

1 cup sugar
1 teaspoon vanilla extract

Preheat oven to 325F (165C). Butter a ridged steamed-pudding mold or a 1-quart straight-sided casserole that has a lid. A charlotte mold also works well. In a large bowl, beat egg, molasses and water. In a medium bowl, thoroughly mix flour, baking powder and baking soda. Place cranberries in a medium bowl. Add 2 tablespoons flour mixture to cranberries; mix until cranberries are well-coated. Stir remaining flour mixture into egg mixture, blending until smooth. Fold in cranberries. Turn into buttered mold. Place in a larger pan. Pour boiling water to a depth of 1 inch in pan. Bake, covered, 2 hours or until a skewer inserted in center comes out clean. While pudding cooks, prepare Frosted Cranberries; set aside. Prepare Caramel Sauce. Serve pudding warm or at room temperature. Unmold warm or cooled pudding onto a serving plate. Pour Caramel Sauce over pudding; garnish with Frosted Cranberries. Makes 6 servings.

Frosted Cranberries:
In a medium bowl, beat egg white until frothy. Brush egg white over cranberries until well-coated. Sprinkle coated cranberries with sugar. Dry completely before using.

Caramel Sauce:
In a medium saucepan, combine butter, cream and sugar. Bring to a boil, stirring constantly. Cook, stirring constantly, about 5 minutes or until syrupy. For a thick golden sauce, cook 5 to 10 minutes. Stir in vanilla. Makes about 1 cup.

Pilgrim's Cranberry Pudding, above; Pumpkin-Almond Pudding, page 147; and Baked Apples with Ginger, page 144.

Noodle Custard

A good, hearty old-fashioned pudding.

3 eggs
1 pint milk (2 cups)
1 cup sugar
1-1/2 teaspoons vanilla extract

2 cups cooked, fine, egg noodles
1/2 cup raisins
1 teaspoon ground nutmeg
Whipped cream, if desired

Preheat oven to 350F (175C). Butter a shallow 3-quart casserole or 13'' x 9'' baking dish. In a large bowl, beat eggs, milk, sugar and vanilla. Stir in cooked noodles and raisins. Turn into buttered casserole. Sprinkle with nutmeg. Bake, covered, 55 minutes to 1 hour or until a knife inserted near center comes out clean. Serve with whipped cream, if desired. Makes 12 servings.

Rice Pudding with Fruit & Honey

Serve this with a fresh-fruit plate for a summer luncheon.

2 cups water
1/2 teaspoon salt
1 cup uncooked medium- or
   long-grain white rice
2 eggs
1 cup milk
1 teaspoon vanilla extract
1/3 cup honey

1/3 cup golden raisins
1/3 cup chopped pitted dates
1 cup diced fresh apple or fresh peach
1/2 cup chopped pecans or walnuts
1/2 teaspoon ground cinnamon
1/4 teaspoon ground nutmeg
1/2 pint whipping cream (1 cup)

Preheat oven to 350F (175C). Butter a shallow 1-1/2-quart casserole or 8-inch-square baking dish. In a medium saucepan, bring water and salt to a boil; stir in rice. Bring back to a boil. Cover and reduce heat to low. Cook 20 to 25 minutes or until rice is tender and has absorbed all the liquid. In a large bowl, beat eggs until frothy; stir in milk, vanilla and honey. Fold in cooked rice, raisins, dates, fresh fruit, nuts, cinnamon and nutmeg. Spread evenly in buttered casserole. Bake, uncovered, 25 minutes, stirring twice to bring mixture from edge of casserole toward center. Pudding will be soft after baking but will stiffen as it cools. Let cool 10 minutes, then stir in cream. Serve immediately or chill. Makes 6 servings.

Springtime Rhubarb Pudding

Make this in the spring when rhubarb is fat and juicy.

8 oz. fresh rhubarb,
    cut in 1-inch pieces (2 cups)
2/3 cup sugar
1 cup all-purpose flour
1-1/2 teaspoons baking powder
1/2 teaspoon salt

1/4 cup butter, room temperature
1/4 cup sugar
1 egg
1/2 teaspoon vanilla extract
1/3 cup milk
Lightly whipped, sweetened cream

Preheat oven to 375F (190C). Butter 6 custard cups or a shallow 1-quart casserole. In a medium bowl, combine rhubarb and 2/3 cup sugar. Divide rhubarb mixture between buttered custard cups or spread evenly in bottom of buttered casserole. In a small bowl, mix flour, baking powder and salt. In a medium bowl, beat butter and 1/4 cup sugar until smooth. Beat in egg until light and lemon-colored. Add flour mixture alternately with vanilla and milk, beating to make a smooth batter. Divide batter over top of rhubarb, spreading evenly. Bake, uncovered, 30 minutes or until golden. Serve warm with lightly whipped, sweetened cream. Makes 6 servings.

Canadian Blueberry Pudding

Wonderful with wild blueberries, but fresh or frozen will do too.

4 cups fresh or frozen blueberries
1/3 cup granulated sugar
2 teaspoons lemon juice
1/4 cup butter, room temperature
1/3 cup packed brown sugar

1/3 cup all-purpose flour
3/4 cup regular or
    quick-cooking rolled oats
Lightly whipped, sweetened cream

Preheat oven to 375F (190C). Butter a shallow 1-1/2-quart casserole or 8-inch-square baking dish. Pour blueberries into casserole in an even layer. Sprinkle with granulated sugar and lemon juice. In a medium bowl, beat butter; beat in brown sugar. Using a fork, blend in flour and oats until mixture is crumbly. Spread over blueberries. Bake, uncovered, 35 to 40 minutes or until crumb topping is browned. Serve hot or at room temperature with lightly whipped, sweetened cream. Makes 6 servings.

Angel in a Casserole   *Photo on page 155.*

This crisp meringue makes a luscious dessert when smothered with fresh fruit and whipped cream!

5 egg whites, room temperature
1 teaspoon salt
1-1/2 cups sugar

1 tablespoon white-wine vinegar
Fresh fruit
Whipped cream, if desired

Preheat oven to 350F (175C). Generously butter a deep 1-1/2-quart soufflé dish or casserole; dust with fine, dry, cake crumbs. In a large bowl, beat egg whites and salt with an electric mixer until foamy. Turn speed to high and add sugar, 1 tablespoon at a time, until 3/4 cup has been added. Beat in vinegar. Continue beating in sugar until mixture is smooth, glossy and holds firm peaks. Turn into prepared dish. Bake, uncovered, 30 minutes, then reduce heat to 250F (120C) and bake 1 hour longer. Cool in dish. Serve with fresh fruit and whipped cream, if desired. Makes 6 servings.

Note: If humidity is high in your kitchen, the meringue will not be crisp and dry. If meringue was baked to crisp-dry stage on 1 day and held in humid conditions, it will absorb moisture from the air and become sticky. Do not attempt to make or store a crisp meringue on a humid day.

Jamaican Lime Pudding

On the northwest coast of Jamaica, limes are abundant!

1/4 cup sugar
1/4 cup all-purpose flour
1/2 teaspoon ground cinnamon
Pinch of salt
2 eggs, separated

1 egg white
3 tablespoons dark Jamaica rum
Grated peel of 1 lime
3 tablespoons lime juice
1 cup half and half

Preheat oven to 375F (190C). Butter a 1-quart soufflé dish or casserole; lightly dust with some sugar. In a medium bowl, mix 1/4 cup sugar, flour, cinnamon and salt; set aside. In another medium bowl, beat 3 egg whites until soft peaks form. In a small bowl, beat egg yolks, rum, lime peel and lime juice. Add egg-yolk mixture and half and half alternately to flour mixture, stirring until well-blended. Fold in beaten egg whites. Pour into prepared dish. Bake, uncovered, 25 to 30 minutes or until set. Serve immediately. Makes 4 servings.

How to Make Angel in a Casserole

1/Turn beaten egg-white mixture into dish. Bake 30 minutes, then reduce heat and bake 1 hour longer.

2/Cool dessert in dish. Serve with fresh fruit and whipped cream, if desired.

Fruit Compote with Star Anise

Star anise adds a pleasant licorice flavor and aroma.

1 (12-oz.) pkg. mixed dried fruit
1 cup golden raisins
1/3 cup sugar
3 cups white wine, white-grape juice or
    water

1 lemon
1 orange
1 (3-inch) cinnamon stick
3 whole star-anise pods
Dairy sour cream

Preheat oven to 300F (150C). Combine mixed dried fruit, raisins, sugar and wine, juice or water in a 2-quart casserole. Using a potato peeler, peel off colored part from lemon and orange in large pieces; place peel on top of fruit mixture. Add cinnamon stick and star-anise pods. Juice lemon and orange; pour juice over fruit mixture. Bake, covered, 1-1/4 hours. Remove and discard peel, cinnamon stick and star-anise pods from fruit. Cool and refrigerate. Serve with sour cream. Makes 6 servings.

German-Chocolate Soufflé

Bring this to the table to be served the moment it is done!

1 (4-oz.) bar German sweet chocolate
1 tablespoon instant coffee granules
5 tablespoons water
1/3 cup all-purpose flour
1 cup cold milk
1 teaspoon vanilla extract

4 egg yolks
8 egg whites, room temperature
1/8 teaspoon cream of tartar
1/2 cup granulated sugar
Powdered sugar
Lightly whipped cream

Preheat oven to 375F (190C). Butter a 2-1/2-quart soufflé dish; lightly dust with granulated sugar. Break chocolate bar into pieces. In a small saucepan or metal bowl, combine chocolate, coffee granules and water. Place over hot water; stir until chocolate is melted. Keep warm. In another small saucepan, combine flour and milk; whisk vigorously until blended. Cook, whisking constantly, over medium-high heat 5 to 10 minutes or until thickened and smooth; remove from heat. Whisk in vanilla and chocolate mixture. Add egg yolks, 1 at a time, whisking to keep mixture smooth. Sauce may be prepared to this point, covered and refrigerated up to 24 hours. In a large bowl, beat egg whites and cream of tartar until white and frothy. Slowly beat in granulated sugar until soft peaks form. Stir about 1/4 of egg-white mixture into sauce to lighten it, then pour sauce onto remaining egg-white mixture. Fold together carefully but not completely; mixture should look marbled. Pour into prepared soufflé dish. Mixture may be prepared to this point and kept at room temperature up to 2 hours before baking. Bake, uncovered, 25 to 30 minutes or until soufflé is high and light but still moves when dish is tapped on the side. Do not overbake unless you do not want a soft center. Sprinkle with powdered sugar and serve immediately with whipped cream. Makes 6 servings.

Baked Chocolate-Cinnamon Fondue

This is an easy, controlled way to melt chocolate for fondue!

1 (12-oz.) bar milk chocolate or
  1 (12-oz.) pkg. milk chocolate or
  semisweet chocolate pieces
3/4 cup whipping cream
1/4 teaspoon ground cinnamon
3 tablespoons rum, Cointreau or
  fruit-flavored liqueur

Bananas, cut in 1-inch chunks;
  pineapple chunks; strawberries;
  cherries; grapes
Pound cake or angel food cake, cut in cubes

Preheat oven to 325F (165C). Break chocolate bar into pieces. In a deep 1-quart casserole, combine chocolate, cream and cinnamon. Bake, uncovered, 25 to 30 minutes or until chocolate is soft. Stir to blend. Stir in rum or liqueur. Place over a candle warmer. Surround with bowls of fresh fruit or cake cubes for dipping. Makes 6 to 8 servings.

Angel in a Casserole, page 152.

Norwegian Lemon Custard

When this bakes, it separates into a spongecake-topped custard.

2 tablespoons butter, room temperature
1 cup sugar
3 eggs, separated
1/4 cup all-purpose flour

1/4 teaspoon salt
1/3 cup lemon juice
1 tablespoon grated lemon peel
1-1/2 cups half and half or whole milk

Preheat oven to 350F (175C). Butter a 1-quart casserole or 6 custard cups. In a medium bowl, beat butter, sugar and egg yolks until light. Add flour, salt, lemon juice and peel. Fold in half and half or milk. In a large bowl, beat egg whites until soft peaks form. Fold into egg-yolk mixture. Pour batter into casserole or divide between custard cups. Place in a larger pan. Pour boiling water to a depth of 1 inch in pan. Bake, uncovered, 30 to 40 minutes or until top is lightly browned. Makes 6 servings.

Creamy Baked Custard

To be sure of a creamy custard, do not overbake it!

4 eggs
1/2 cup sugar
1/4 teaspoon salt

1 teaspoon vanilla extract
1 pint whipping cream (2 cups)
1 pint milk (2 cups)

Preheat oven to 350F (175C). Butter a 1-1/2-quart casserole. In a medium bowl, beat eggs, sugar, salt and vanilla. In a medium saucepan, heat cream and milk over low heat until small bubbles form around side of pan. Stir into egg mixture. Strain into buttered casserole. Place in a larger pan. Pour boiling water to a depth of 1 inch in pan. Bake, uncovered, 30 minutes or until a knife inserted in center comes out clean. Makes 6 servings.

Variations

Almond Custard: Halfway through baking, sprinkle custard with 1/2 cup sliced almonds.
Black-Bottomed Custard: Sprinkle bottom of buttered casserole with 1 cup chocolate pieces before adding egg mixture. Carefully strain egg mixture over chocolate pieces so they remain on bottom of casserole.
Caramel Custard: Sprinkle bottom of buttered casserole with 1/2 cup packed brown sugar. Carefully strain egg mixture over sugar.

Index

Metric Chart

Comparison to Metric Measure

When You Know	Symbol	Multiply By	To Find	Symbol
teaspoons	tsp	5.0	milliliters	ml
tablespoons	tbsp	15.0	milliliters	ml
fluid ounces	fl. oz.	30.0	milliliters	ml
cups	c	0.24	liters	l
pints	pt.	0.47	liters	l
quarts	qt.	0.95	liters	l
ounces	oz.	28.0	grams	g
pounds	lb.	0.45	kilograms	kg
Fahrenheit	F	5/9 (after subtracting 32)	Celsius	C

Liquid Measure to Liters

1/4 cup	=	0.06 liters
1/2 cup	=	0.12 liters
3/4 cup	=	0.18 liters
1 cup	=	0.24 liters
1-1/4 cups	=	0.3 liters
1-1/2 cups	=	0.36 liters
2 cups	=	0.48 liters
2-1/2 cups	=	0.6 liters
3 cups	=	0.72 liters
3-1/2 cups	=	0.84 liters
4 cups	=	0.96 liters
4-1/2 cups	=	1.08 liters
5 cups	=	1.2 liters
5-1/2 cups	=	1.32 liters

Liquid Measure to Milliliters

1/4 teaspoon	=	1.25 milliliters
1/2 teaspoon	=	2.5 milliliters
3/4 teaspoon	=	3.75 milliliters
1 teaspoon	=	5.0 milliliters
1-1/4 teaspoons	=	6.25 milliliters
1-1/2 teaspoons	=	7.5 milliliters
1-3/4 teaspoons	=	8.75 milliliters
2 teaspoons	=	10.0 milliliters
1 tablespoon	=	15.0 milliliters
2 tablespoons	=	30.0 milliliters